EXPAT GUIDE: PORTUGAL

The essential guide to becoming an expatriate in Portugal

©2023 JASON KILHOFFER

Expat Guide: Portugal
Copyright © 2023, Jason Kilhoffer
All rights reserved.
Published by Jason Kilhoffer
ISBN: 978-1-0878-7822-5
Library of Congress Cataloging-in-Publication Data
Kilhoffer, Jason. Expat Guide: Portugal.
Edition: First Edition
Cover Design by: Jason Kilhoffer
Interior Layout by: Jason Kilhoffer
Printed in United State of America

Disclaimer
General Information Only: The information provided in this book is for general informational purposes only. It should not be considered as professional advice on any subject matter.
No Professional Relationship: Reading this book does not create any professional relationship between the reader and the author or publisher.
Accuracy of Information: While every effort has been made to ensure that the information contained in this book is accurate and up to date, the author and publisher make no representations or warranties of any kind, express or implied, about the completeness, accuracy, reliability, suitability, or availability of the content.
Liability Limitation: In no event will the author or publisher be liable for any loss or damage including without limitation, indirect or consequential loss or damage, or any loss or damage whatsoever arising from loss of data or profits arising out of, or in connection with, the use of this book.
External Links: Any links to external websites provided within this book are provided for the reader's convenience only. The author and publisher have no control over the content of these sites and accept no responsibility for them or for any loss or damage that may arise from the reader's use of them.
Professional Advice: The information contained in this book is not intended to replace professional advice. If the reader requires professional advice in relation to any matter, he or she should consult an appropriately qualified professional.
Changes to Content: The author and publisher reserve the right to make changes to the content, layout, and other elements of this book without notice.

No part of this publication may be reproduced, stored in a retrieval system, or transmitted in any form or by any means, electronic, mechanical, photocopying, recording, or otherwise, without written permission of the publisher.
https://expatguideseries.com
expatguideseries@gmail.com

Contents

- Map of Portugal 6
- 1. Introduction 7
  - 1.1 Brief Overview of Portugal 7
  - 1.2 Why an Expat Guide for Portugal? 8
  - 1.3 Myths and Misconceptions about Portugal 9
- 2. Understanding Expat Life 12
  - 2.1 What is an Expat? 12
  - 2.2 The Expat Journey: Stages and Transitions 13
  - 2.3 Benefits and Challenges of Being an Expat 15
- 3. Why Choose Portugal? 18
  - 3.1 Geography and Climate of Portugal 18
  - 3.2 Culture and Heritage of Portugal 20
  - 3.3 Cost of Living in Portugal 22
  - 3.4 Safety and Security Considerations in Portugal 23
  - 3.5 Political and Socioeconomic Climate in Portugal 25
  - 3.6 Comparisons with Other Popular Expat Destinations 27
  - 3.7 Ecological Diversity and Outdoor Activities in Portugal 28
- 4. Legal Considerations 31
  - 4.1 Visa Types and Application Process in Portugal 31
  - 4.2 Work Permits in Portugal 33
  - 4.3 Renewal and Long-term Stay Considerations in Portugal 35

- 4.4 Requirements for Permanent Residency and Citizenship in Portugal 37
- 4.5 Legal Rights and Responsibilities in Portugal 39

5. Health and Insurance 42
    - 5.1 Healthcare System in Portugal 42
    - 5.2 Health Insurance Options in Portugal 44
    - 5.3 Vaccinations and Preventive Care in Portugal 45
    - 5.4 Dealing with Medical Emergencies in Portugal 47
    - 5.5 Mental Health Resources in Portugal 48

6. Housing and Accommodation 51
    - 6.1 Renting vs. Buying in Portugal 51
    - 6.2 Typical Housing Costs in Portugal 53
    - 6.3 Choosing a Location in Portugal 55
    - 6.4 Utilities and Other Expenses in Portugal 56
    - 6.5 Land and Property Laws for Expats in Portugal 58

7. Cost of Living 61
    - 7.1 Typical Monthly Expenses in Portugal 61
    - 7.2 Cost of Food and Groceries in Portugal 63
    - 7.3 Cost of Transportation in Portugal 64
    - 7.4 Leisure and Entertainment Costs in Portugal 66
    - 7.5 Tax Considerations in Portugal 67

8. Education 70
    - 8.1 Overview of the Education System in Portugal 70
    - 8.2 International and Local Schools in Portugal 72
    - 8.3 Schooling Options for Expat Children in Portugal 73

- 8.4 Adult and Continuing Education Opportunities in Portugal 75
- 8.5 Learning Languages in Portugal..............................76

9. Work and Business 79
- 9.1 Employment Opportunities and Job Market Overview in Portugal..................79
- 9.2 Professional Qualifications and Certifications in Portugal 81
- 9.3 Starting a Business in Portugal 82
- 9.4 Labor Laws and Employee Rights in Portugal..........84
- 9.5 Income Tax Considerations in Portugal....................86
- 9.6 Networking and Professional Groups in Portugal 87

10. Language and Culture....................................90
- 10.1 Local Languages in Portugal................................90
- 10.2 Cultural Norms and Etiquette in Portugal 91
- 10.3 Holidays and Festivals in Portugal 93
- 10.4 Integrating into the Local Community in Portugal ...94
- 10.5 Religion and Its Role in Portuguese Culture...........96

11. Practical Information 98
- 11.1 Transportation System in Portugal 98
- 11.2 Internet and Telecommunications in Portugal.......100
- 11.3 Local Cuisine in Portugal.....................................101
- 11.4 Safety and Security Tips in Portugal....................103
- 11.5 Shopping and Food in Portugal............................105
- 11.6 Pet Ownership and Animal Laws in Portugal........106

12. Life as an Expat 109

12.1 Expat Communities in Portugal............................ 109

12.2 Making Local Friends in Portugal......................... 111

12.3 Dealing with Homesickness in Portugal 113

12.4 Benefits and Challenges Specific to Portugal....... 114

13. Planning the Move 118

13.1 Timeline and Checklist for Moving to Portugal 118

13.2 What to Bring When Moving to Portugal 121

13.3 Hiring a Moving Company for Portugal................. 122

13.4 Banking Considerations for Moving to Portugal.... 124

13.5 Customs Regulations for Moving to Portugal 126

13.6 Notifying Home Country Government Agencies... 128

13.7 Relocation Services and Their Benefits................ 129

Map of Portugal

1. Introduction

1.1 Brief Overview of Portugal

Located in southwestern Europe on the Iberian Peninsula, Portugal is a country known for its rich cultural heritage, beautiful landscapes, and favorable climate. Portugal is the westernmost country of mainland Europe and is bordered by the Atlantic Ocean to the west and south and by Spain to the north and east. The country includes the archipelagos of Madeira and the Azores in the Atlantic Ocean.

Portugal's capital and largest city is Lisbon, and other major cities include Porto, Vila Nova de Gaia, and Amadora. The official language is Portuguese, and the country has a population of approximately 10 million people.

Portugal is a member of the United Nations and the European Union. It uses the euro (€) as its currency. It has a diverse economy with strong sectors in services, manufacturing, and agriculture. The country is known for its production of wine, olive oil, and cork.

Portugal's history dates to prehistoric times, but it emerged as a significant global power during the Age of Discovery in the 15th and 16th centuries when Portuguese explorers like Vasco da Gama established sea routes to India, Africa, and the Americas. This history is reflected in the country's rich architecture, traditions, and culture.

In recent years, Portugal has become a popular destination for expats due to its comfortable climate, friendly locals, high quality of life, and affordable cost of living. Its geographical diversity ranges from mountainous regions in the north, characterized by vineyards and rolling hills, to the picturesque beaches in the southern region known as the Algarve.

Whether it's the vibrant city life of Lisbon and Porto, the quiet countryside, or the appealing beaches, Portugal offers a unique blend of lifestyle options that are attractive to expats from around the globe.

1.2 Why an Expat Guide for Portugal?

The decision to become an expat and move to a new country is a significant one, filled with both excitement and uncertainty. Portugal, with its rich cultural heritage, inviting climate, and welcoming locals, has become a preferred destination for many expats. However, understanding the nuances of life in

Portugal, from its bureaucratic procedures to cultural norms, is essential for a smooth transition.

This guide aims to serve as a comprehensive resource for anyone considering the move. It delves into the details of the Portuguese lifestyle, legal and health considerations, housing, cost of living, and more. While the internet is inundated with information, not all of it is accurate, up-to-date, or practical. This guide aims to provide reliable and pragmatic advice to help potential expats navigate through these complex areas.

Furthermore, we understand that everyone's expat journey is unique. Whether you're a retiree looking for a peaceful coastal town, a digital nomad seeking a vibrant city with reliable internet, or a family looking for a safe environment with quality education for your children, this guide aims to equip you with the knowledge to make informed decisions that suit your individual needs and lifestyle preferences.

In essence, this guide is designed to bridge the gap between contemplating the move to Portugal and executing it, providing practical advice and insider tips, debunking common misconceptions, and giving you a clear view of what to expect. Moving to a new country can be a challenging process, but with the right information and preparation, it can also be an enriching and fulfilling adventure.

1.3 Myths and Misconceptions about Portugal

Like any country, Portugal is the subject of several myths and misconceptions that can influence the perceptions of those looking to relocate. It is important to debunk these myths to provide a realistic picture of what living in Portugal is like.

1. **Portugal is a poor country:** While Portugal is not one of the wealthiest countries in Europe, it is far from poor. The quality of life is high, and it has a well-developed infrastructure, a good education system, and a robust healthcare system. Portugal also consistently ranks as one of the world's safest countries.

2. **Everyone in Portugal speaks English:** Although English is widely spoken, especially in the tourist areas and among the younger population, not everyone in Portugal speaks English. It's essential to try to learn Portuguese to fully integrate into the local culture and community.

3. **Portugal's climate is always hot:** Portugal has a Mediterranean climate, with hot summers and mild winters in the coastal areas. However, the weather can significantly vary depending on the region. The northern parts of Portugal can be quite rainy and cold in winter, while the central interior can experience very cold temperatures and even snow.

4. **Portugal is just beach resorts:** Portugal has more to offer than just beach resorts. From historic cities like Lisbon and Porto, to the beautiful vineyards in the Douro Valley, to mountain ranges and national parks, Portugal is a country of diverse landscapes and cultural experiences.

5. **Portuguese food is all about seafood:** While Portugal, with its extensive coastline, is famous for its seafood, the country's cuisine is incredibly diverse. It includes a variety of meats, cheeses, and a wide range

of desserts. Each region in Portugal has its distinct culinary traditions and specialties.

6. **Living in Portugal is like being on a constant vacation:** Living in Portugal is not the same as being on holiday. Although the quality of life is high, expats still need to navigate daily tasks, bureaucracy, and the occasional culture shock. It's essential to have realistic expectations and prepare for the practical aspects of life in Portugal.

Understanding the reality behind these misconceptions is key to making an informed decision about moving to Portugal. Through this guide, we hope to present a balanced and realistic view of life in Portugal, enabling potential expats to plan their move with confidence and excitement.

2. Understanding Expat Life

2.1 What is an Expat?

An expatriate, commonly referred to as an expat, is a person who has chosen to live outside their native country. This decision can be motivated by a variety of reasons such as employment opportunities, study, retirement, adventure, or the desire for a different lifestyle or cultural experience.

Expats come from all walks of life and represent a broad spectrum of professions, ages, and backgrounds. They could be corporate employees assigned to a foreign office, entrepreneurs establishing a business abroad, students studying in international institutions, retirees settling in a warmer climate, or digital nomads working remotely while exploring different cultures.

It's important to note that being an expat is not just about physical relocation but also cultural adaptation. Expats often need to navigate a new language, customs, and social norms, which can be both challenging and rewarding. This journey involves not only adapting to a new environment but also understanding and appreciating the host country's culture and lifestyle.

Living as an expat can provide a rich and transformative experience. It offers the opportunity to develop new skills, gain global perspectives, build diverse relationships, and discover new facets of one's identity. However, it's also a journey that requires preparation, open-mindedness, and resilience, all of which we will explore further in this guide.

While the term expat is used widely, it's worth noting that it is sometimes critiqued for being applied differently to people depending on factors such as their country of origin or economic status. In this guide, we use the term to refer to anyone living outside their home country, regardless of their specific circumstances.

2.2 The Expat Journey: Stages and Transitions

The expat journey is a transformative process with distinct stages, each with its own unique characteristics, challenges, and transitions. Understanding these stages can provide a helpful framework for navigating your move to Portugal.

1. **Research and Decision Making:** This is the first stage where you're contemplating the move, weighing the pros and cons, and gathering information. It involves significant research about Portugal, including its culture, cost of living, legalities, and lifestyle. Making the decision to become an expat involves a mix of excitement, anxiety, and anticipation.

2. **Preparation and Departure:** Once the decision is made, the focus shifts to logistical preparations. This includes securing visas, finding accommodation, arranging health insurance, packing, and saying goodbye to friends and family. This stage can be filled with a flurry of activities and emotions.

3. **Arrival and Adjustment:** Upon arriving in Portugal, expats often experience a 'honeymoon period' characterized by enthusiasm and curiosity. This stage involves adjusting to the new surroundings, language, cuisine, and customs. It can also involve practical tasks such as setting up a bank account, getting a phone number, and registering with local authorities.

4. **Adaptation and Integration:** As the initial excitement fades, the reality of daily life sets in. This stage may present challenges as you encounter cultural differences, language barriers, and perhaps feelings of homesickness. However, it's also a time of deepening understanding of the local culture, building relationships, and establishing routines.

5. **Stability and Belonging:** Over time, as you become more familiar and comfortable with Portuguese life, you will transition into a stage of stability. Portugal will start

to feel like home, and you will likely experience a sense of belonging and familiarity.

6. **Repatriation or Moving On:** For some, the expat journey might eventually lead to a return to their home country, which comes with its own set of adjustments. Others might decide to move to a new country and embark on a new expat journey.

Remember, these stages are not always linear, and everyone's journey is unique. Some stages might take longer than others, and challenges might arise when least expected. Being aware of these stages can help you prepare mentally and emotionally, allowing for a smoother and more enjoyable expat experience in Portugal.

2.3 Benefits and Challenges of Being an Expat

Living as an expat in Portugal, like any country, comes with its own unique set of benefits and challenges. Understanding these can provide a well-rounded perspective and help manage expectations.

Benefits:

1. **Cultural Exposure:** Living in Portugal exposes you to a new culture, traditions, and ways of life. It offers a chance to learn a new language, try new cuisines, and understand different worldviews.

2. **Personal Growth:** The expat experience often promotes personal growth. It can boost your

adaptability, resilience, problem-solving skills, and ability to communicate across cultural boundaries. It can also lead to increased self-awareness and independence.

3. **Career Opportunities:** Portugal is home to a vibrant startup scene and offers various opportunities for entrepreneurs. There are also opportunities for teaching English, tourism, real estate, and more. For some, living abroad can enhance their CV, providing a competitive edge in an increasingly globalized job market.

4. **Quality of Life:** Portugal consistently ranks high for quality of life. It offers a relaxed pace of life, a pleasant climate, beautiful landscapes, rich history, and a lower cost of living compared to many Western countries. The healthcare system is also well-regarded.

5. **Community:** There is a sizable and welcoming expat community in Portugal. This can provide a supportive network as you navigate your new surroundings.

Challenges:

1. **Cultural Differences:** Understanding and adjusting to cultural nuances can take time. Portugal, like any country, has its own customs, social norms, and traditions that may be different from what you're used to.

2. **Language Barrier:** While many Portuguese speak English, especially in the cities and amongst the younger generation, not knowing Portuguese can limit

your ability to fully integrate or handle certain bureaucratic tasks.

3. **Bureaucracy:** Portugal, like many Southern European countries, is known for its bureaucratic processes. Whether it's dealing with visas, setting up utilities, or navigating the healthcare system, be prepared for paperwork.

4. **Homesickness:** Moving to a new country often means leaving behind familiar surroundings, family, and friends. Even in the age of digital communication, homesickness can be a common challenge.

5. **Costs:** While Portugal is often lauded for its affordable cost of living, initial setup costs can be high, especially if you're renting or buying property, shipping belongings, or setting up a business.

Being an expat is a complex, enriching, and challenging journey. By understanding the potential benefits and challenges, you can make an informed decision and prepare for a successful move to Portugal.

3. Why Choose Portugal?

3.1 Geography and Climate of Portugal

Portugal, located on the Iberian Peninsula in Southwestern Europe, is known for its diverse and stunning landscapes. From pristine beaches to dramatic mountain ranges, charming villages to cosmopolitan cities, Portugal offers a wide range of geographical features that attract expats from around the world.

Portugal can be divided into several regions, each with its unique characteristics:

1. **Northern Portugal:** This region is home to the country's second-largest city, Porto, renowned for its

historic center, port wine, and vibrant cultural scene. The north also encompasses the lush Minho region, known for Vinho Verde (green wine), and the mountainous Trás-os-Montes.

2. **Central Portugal:** The central region includes Coimbra, a city known for its prestigious university, and the mountainous Serra da Estrela, the highest mainland points in Portugal. The region also contains vast pine forests and pristine river beaches.
3. **Lisbon and Surroundings:** The capital city, Lisbon, is famous for its rich history, iconic tram network, and the nearby fairy-tale town of Sintra. To the west, you'll find Estoril and Cascais, popular seaside towns known for their beaches and luxury resorts.

4. **Alentejo:** This large region stretches from the Tagus River down to the Algarve and is characterized by its rolling plains, cork oak forests, vineyards, and historical cities like Évora.

5. **Algarve:** Located in the south, the Algarve is renowned for its stunning coastline, picturesque fishing towns, golf courses, and as a popular destination for tourists and expat retirees.

6. **Islands:** Portugal also includes the archipelagos of Madeira and the Azores. These volcanic islands offer a subtropical climate, unique landscapes, and are popular with nature lovers.

Portugal's climate varies from north to south. The north has a temperate maritime climate with cool, rainy winters and warm, dry summers. Central Portugal experiences hot summers and cold winters, especially in the higher altitudes. Lisbon and the Alentejo region enjoy a Mediterranean climate with hot summers and mild, rainy winters, while the Algarve has the warmest weather in Portugal, with mild, rainy winters and long, hot summers.

Understanding the geographical diversity and climate of Portugal can help you choose the region that best suits your lifestyle preferences and climate tolerance when planning your move.

3.2 Culture and Heritage of Portugal

Portugal boasts a rich cultural heritage shaped by a history of diverse influences, from the Celts and Romans to the Moors and Christians. Its strategic geographical location on the Atlantic coast of the Iberian Peninsula has led to a culture of exploration and discovery, as evidenced by the Age of Exploration in the 15th and 16th centuries when Portuguese explorers like Vasco da Gama charted new sea routes and made significant contributions to global trade and interaction.

Portuguese culture is grounded in a love for tradition, community, and hospitality. It is reflected in the country's well-preserved historic architecture, engaging festivals, delicious cuisine, and distinctive music, such as Fado, the soulful folk music recognized by UNESCO as a World Heritage tradition.

Language: The official language of Portugal is Portuguese. While English is commonly spoken in tourist areas and among the younger population, understanding and speaking Portuguese is vital for integration into local life. Portugal also offers Portuguese language courses geared towards newcomers.

Art and Architecture: Portugal has a diverse array of artistic styles, from Romanesque and Gothic to Manueline and Baroque. The country is also known for azulejos, decorative ceramic tiles adorning buildings inside and out. Portugal's UNESCO World Heritage Sites, such as the Monastery of Batalha, the Cultural Landscape of Sintra, and the Historic Centre of Porto, are testaments to its rich architectural heritage.

Cuisine: Portuguese cuisine is hearty and diverse, with a heavy emphasis on fresh seafood, such as bacalhau (salted cod), sardines, and shellfish. Meat dishes like feijoada (bean stew with pork) and cozido à portuguesa (Portuguese boiled dinner) are also popular. Portugal is also known for its pastries, particularly pastel de nata (custard tart), and its variety of wines, including Vinho Verde, Port, and Madeira.

Festivals and Celebrations: Portugal hosts numerous festivals throughout the year. The most well-known is probably the Festa de São João in Porto, an overnight street festival every June celebrating Saint John the Baptist with grilled sardines, folk dances, and firework displays. The Feast of the Trays in Tomar, featuring a procession of hundreds of women carrying towering trays of bread and flowers on their heads, is another unique event.

Sports: Football (soccer) is a national passion in Portugal, which has produced world-renowned players like Cristiano Ronaldo and Eusébio. The Portuguese also enjoy a range of other sports, including futsal, roller hockey, and athletics. Overall, Portugal's culture and heritage offer a rich tapestry of experiences and opportunities for learning and integration. It's a place where the modern and the traditional coexist, creating a vibrant cultural scene that is both fascinating and endearing.

3.3 Cost of Living in Portugal

One of the significant attractions for expats considering Portugal is its relatively low cost of living compared to many other Western European countries. However, like any location, the cost of living can vary widely based on your lifestyle choices and the region in which you choose to live.

Housing: Housing tends to be quite affordable, particularly when compared to cities like Paris, London, or Berlin. The cost of housing varies across regions with Lisbon, Porto, and the Algarve being the most expensive. However, even in these areas, the prices are likely to be cheaper than in many major European and North American cities. The further inland or into the less-populated areas you go, the cheaper the property prices.

Groceries: Food and groceries in Portugal are relatively inexpensive, especially local produce, dairy products, and bakery items. Portugal is also famous for its wines, which are excellent and often surprisingly affordable.

Dining and Entertainment: Eating out at restaurants is also quite reasonable, particularly if you stick to local establishments and Portuguese cuisine. The cost of entertainment, such as cinema, theater, and concerts, is generally lower than in many other European countries.

Utilities and Services: Utility costs, such as electricity, water, and internet, can vary depending on the size of your property and usage. However, they tend to be relatively affordable compared to many other Western countries.

Transportation: Public transportation in Portugal is reliable and inexpensive, with extensive bus and metro services in the larger cities and a good network of trains connecting towns across the country. Owning a car can be more costly, with relatively high prices for vehicles, fuel, and toll roads.

Healthcare: While healthcare costs in Portugal are generally lower than in many other developed countries, it's essential for expats to secure appropriate health insurance. Expats from certain countries with reciprocal healthcare agreements can access the Portuguese National Health Service (SNS) at low cost.

Despite its affordability, it's essential to remember that wages and salaries in Portugal are also lower than in many other parts of Europe. As an expat, it's crucial to thoroughly research and budget for the cost of living in your chosen region of Portugal to ensure a comfortable and sustainable lifestyle.

3.4 Safety and Security Considerations in Portugal

When moving to a new country, understanding the safety and security landscape is vital. Fortunately, Portugal is considered one of the safest countries in the world. The Global Peace Index consistently ranks Portugal highly for its low crime rates and political stability.

General Safety: Portugal has a low rate of violent crime. Petty crime like pickpocketing and car break-ins do occur, especially in tourist areas and larger cities like Lisbon and Porto, but they are less frequent than in many other European cities.

Road Safety: While Portugal has made considerable improvements in road safety over the years, the accident rate is still higher than the European average. This is often attributed to aggressive driving habits. If you plan to drive in Portugal, ensure you understand the local driving laws and always exercise caution, especially on unfamiliar roads.

Natural Disasters: Portugal is relatively safe from severe natural disasters. The country does experience occasional minor earthquakes, and forest fires can occur in rural areas, particularly in the hot, dry summer months. However, these incidents are usually localized and well-handled by authorities.

Political Stability: Portugal enjoys a high level of political stability. Protests and demonstrations do occur, as they do in any democracy, but they are generally peaceful and well-regulated by local authorities.

Health and Medical Services: Portugal has a good standard of healthcare. The World Health Organization ranks Portugal's health system higher than countries like the United States, Canada, and Australia. However, expats should have comprehensive health insurance to access private healthcare services.

Emergency Services: In the event of an emergency, the number to call is 112, the European standard emergency number, which can be dialed free of charge from any telephone or mobile phone.

As with any location, while living in Portugal, it's essential to exercise common sense and take precautions to safeguard your personal security and belongings. This includes actions like locking your home and car, not leaving belongings unattended, and avoiding less secure areas late at night. However, the overall risk level in Portugal is comparatively low, making it a safe and comfortable choice for many expats.

3.5 Political and Socioeconomic Climate in Portugal

Understanding the political and socioeconomic climate of a country is crucial for expats as it can significantly influence aspects like quality of life, stability, and access to public services.

Political Climate: Portugal is a democratic republic with a stable political environment. It's a parliamentary system where the President is the head of state, and the Prime Minister is the head of government. Portugal is part of the European Union, which means it adheres to the standards and regulations of the EU.

Socioeconomic Climate: Portugal has a mixed economy, with both public and private sectors playing significant roles. Its economy is characterized by a diverse range of industries, including manufacturing, services, and agriculture. However, it's worth noting that while Portugal has been steadily recovering from the severe recession it experienced due to the financial crisis in 2008, the average wage is still lower than in many other Western European countries.

Employment: The job market in Portugal is relatively stable, although the unemployment rate can fluctuate. Key sectors that drive the Portuguese economy include the service sector (notably tourism), manufacturing (especially automotive and aerospace), agriculture, and fishing. Portugal's digital and tech startup scene is also growing, creating new opportunities for foreign professionals.

Social Services: Portugal has a comprehensive welfare system, which includes healthcare, education, and social security. Public healthcare and education are available to all residents, but many expats opt for private services due to shorter waiting times and often higher standards.

Public Sentiment: The Portuguese people are generally welcoming and friendly towards foreigners. There is a strong sense of community and family values are highly respected. However, learning the language can significantly improve an expat's experience as it aids in integrating into Portuguese society.

Foreign Relations: Portugal maintains positive relations with countries around the globe due to its historical ties as a seafaring nation and a key player in the Age of Discovery. Its membership in the European Union, NATO, and United Nations also contributes to its global standing.

Overall, Portugal offers a stable political and socioeconomic environment, making it an attractive destination for expats. As with any country, it's always beneficial to keep abreast of current affairs and understand the broader context in which you are living.

3.6 Comparisons with Other Popular Expat Destinations

When considering a move to Portugal, it's useful to compare it with other popular expat destinations to help decide if it's the right choice for you. Here are some key considerations:

Cost of Living: As mentioned earlier, Portugal boasts a significantly lower cost of living compared to other popular expat destinations like France, Germany, or the UK. The cost of housing, groceries, dining, and entertainment are typically cheaper than most Western European nations.

Quality of Life: Portugal consistently ranks high in quality-of-life indexes. This is due to factors such as a pleasant climate, safe environment, and a laid-back lifestyle.

Healthcare: Portugal's healthcare system is well-regarded and is ranked above many other countries by the World Health Organization. While some popular expat destinations like the United States have high healthcare costs, Portugal provides high-quality healthcare services at a relatively lower cost.

Work-Life Balance: Portugal is known for its relaxed pace of life and emphasis on enjoying life, which can be a stark contrast to the high-pressure work environments in cities like London, New York, or Tokyo.

Language Barrier: Portugal is a non-English speaking country, but English is commonly understood, especially among the younger population and in tourist areas. This can make it easier to settle in compared to countries where English is less widely spoken.

Climate: Portugal enjoys a Mediterranean climate, with hot summers and mild winters. This can be a significant draw compared to countries with harsh winters or extremely hot summers.

Ease of Travel: Portugal's location in Southwestern Europe makes it a great base for exploring the rest of Europe and Northern Africa. The well-connected airports and its membership in the Schengen Area make travel convenient and straightforward.

Cultural Experiences: Portugal offers a rich tapestry of cultural experiences, from its unique cuisine and wine to its historic architecture and music. While every country offers its cultural experiences, the blend of history, art, and nature in Portugal is particularly appealing to many expats.

Remember, the ideal expat destination depends on individual preferences and circumstances. While Portugal offers many advantages, it's essential to consider what aspects of living abroad are most important to you.

3.7 Ecological Diversity and Outdoor Activities in Portugal

Portugal, while relatively small, offers an impressive variety of landscapes and ecological diversity, making it an exciting destination for outdoor enthusiasts and nature lovers.

Coastline and Beaches: Portugal boasts a stunning coastline that stretches over 800 kilometers. Its beaches, from the scenic Algarve in the south to the surfing havens around Peniche and Nazaré, are famous worldwide. You'll find everything from vast sandy beaches to secluded coves, perfect for sunbathing, swimming, and watersports.

Mountains and Hiking: For those who prefer the mountains, the rugged peaks of the Serra da Estrela, Portugal's highest mountain range, offers excellent hiking, rock climbing, and even skiing during winter. Other notable areas for hiking include Peneda-Gerês National Park and the scenic trails in Madeira and the Azores islands.

Flora and Fauna: Portugal's diverse landscapes, from cork oak forests in Alentejo to the unique Laurisilva forests in Madeira, are home to a wide variety of plants and wildlife. Bird watchers will appreciate the numerous bird species, especially in protected areas like the Ria Formosa Natural Park and the Tagus Estuary.

Rivers and Lakes: Portugal's rivers, such as the Douro and the Tagus, offer beautiful landscapes and opportunities for activities like canoeing, fishing, or river cruises. The Alqueva, Europe's largest artificial lake, is a dark sky reserve, perfect for stargazing.

Vineyards and Agriculture: The rolling vineyards of the Douro Valley and the Dão region are not only picturesque but also produce some of Portugal's famous wines. Olive groves, almond orchards, and cork forests add to the country's agricultural diversity.

Urban Parks and Gardens: Even within Portugal's cities, you'll find green spaces for outdoor relaxation. The Calouste Gulbenkian Park in Lisbon and the City Park in Porto are great urban escapes.

Cycling and Walking Routes: Portugal has invested in developing cycling and walking routes in recent years. The Portuguese Coastal Camino and the Alentejo Rota Vicentina are two fantastic long-distance trails to explore.

Outdoor activities in Portugal are not only abundant but also accessible year-round due to the country's favorable climate. Whether you're a hiker, cyclist, surfer, or just someone who appreciates being in nature, you'll find something to love in Portugal's great outdoors.

4. Legal Considerations

4.1 Visa Types and Application Process in Portugal

As an expat planning to move to Portugal, it's essential to understand the various types of visas and the application process. Here is an overview:

Schengen Visa (Short-term): If you are from a non-EU country and plan to stay in Portugal for up to 90 days within a 180-day period for purposes like tourism, business, or visiting relatives, you'll likely need a Schengen Visa. This visa also allows travel to other Schengen Area countries.

Residency Visa (Long-term): For a stay longer than three months, you will need to apply for a Residency Visa before you move. This visa is intended for those who wish to work, study, retire, or live long-term in Portugal. It is a two-step process where you initially apply for a visa to enter Portugal for the purpose of requesting a residence permit, and after arrival, you apply for the actual residence permit.

Specific types of Residency Visas include:

1. **Work Visa:** For those who have an employment offer from a Portuguese employer. Your employer will need to obtain an initial approval from the Portuguese authorities.

2. **Golden Visa:** This is for non-EU citizens who make certain types of investment in Portugal, such as buying property worth €500,000 or more, or creating at least 10 jobs.

3. **D7 Visa or Passive Income Visa:** For individuals who can prove they have sufficient funds to support themselves without working, such as retirees or remote workers.

4. **Study Visa:** For international students who are accepted into a Portuguese educational institution.

Non-Habitual Residency (NHR): This is not a visa, but a tax status designed to attract professionals of high cultural and economic worth. It offers tax advantages for your first ten years living in Portugal.

Application Process:

1. **Preparation:** Gather required documents such as your passport, proof of sufficient funds, health insurance, criminal record certificate, and documents showing the purpose of your stay (like a work contract or school enrollment confirmation).

2. **Application:** Submit your application at the Portuguese embassy or consulate in your home country.

3. **Wait:** The processing time can vary greatly, from a few weeks to several months, depending on the type of visa and your nationality.

4. **Arrival in Portugal:** Once you have your visa and arrive in Portugal, you will need to apply for a residence permit if you're staying long-term.

Remember, visa rules can change and depend on your specific circumstances and nationality. Always check with your nearest Portuguese embassy or consulate or use a legal professional's services to guide you through the process.

4.2 Work Permits in Portugal

If you intend to work in Portugal as an expat, understanding the country's work permit regulations is crucial. Here's a brief overview:

For EU/EEA/Switzerland Citizens: If you're from the European Union (EU), European Economic Area (EEA), or

Switzerland, you have the right to live and work in Portugal without a work permit under the freedom of movement principle. You only need to register your residence if you plan to stay in the country longer than three months.

For Non-EU/EEA/Switzerland Citizens: If you're from outside the EU/EEA/Switzerland, you'll need to obtain a work visa, which serves as a work permit, before entering Portugal. This process involves two steps:

1. **Work Contract or Binding Job Offer:** First, you must secure a work contract, or a binding job offer from a Portuguese employer.

2. **Work Visa Application:** The employer will need to request an authorization from the Portuguese Labor Authority (IEFP). Once approved, you can then apply for a work visa (Residence Visa for Work Purposes) from the Portuguese embassy or consulate in your home country.

It's important to note that your work visa and residence permit will only be valid for the job and region specified in your work contract or job offer. If you wish to change jobs or move to a different area, you must notify the immigration authorities.

Once in Portugal, you have up to six months to find a job (if you didn't have a job offer before arrival) and apply for a Residence Permit for Work Purposes. After five years of legal residency in Portugal, you can apply for permanent residency.

For Self-Employed and Entrepreneurs: If you plan to work as a self-employed professional or entrepreneur, you can apply for a different type of visa, known as the D2 Visa or Visa for Immigrant Entrepreneurs.

Remember, the process can be complex and time-consuming, with specific requirements and documents needed. Always check the most current information from official resources or consult with an immigration expert to ensure you follow the correct procedure.

4.3 Renewal and Long-term Stay Considerations in Portugal

Once you have moved to Portugal, it's crucial to understand the process for renewing your residency and considerations for a long-term stay.

Residence Permit Renewal: Temporary residence permits are initially valid for one year and then renewable every two years. To renew your permit, you need to apply to the Immigration and Borders Service (SEF). This should be done 30 days before the expiry of your current permit. For the renewal, you will typically need to present proof of sufficient income, proof of accommodation, and a clean criminal record. After five years of temporary residence, you can apply for a permanent residence permit.

Permanent Residence: After five years of legal residency, you can apply for permanent residency in Portugal. This status provides more stability as it is not subject to regular renewals. However, you still need to meet specific criteria, including proof of sufficient income and basic knowledge of the Portuguese language. Permanent residents also have the same rights and duties as Portuguese citizens, apart from the right to vote or hold public office.

Portuguese Citizenship: After six years of legal residency (one of which can be with a permanent residence permit), you can apply for Portuguese citizenship. This will grant you the same rights as Portuguese citizens, including the ability to live, work, and study anywhere within the EU. Requirements include A2 level proficiency in the Portuguese language and connections to the Portuguese community.

Long-term Stay Considerations:

1. **Integration:** The longer you stay in Portugal, the more important it is to integrate into the local community. This might involve learning the language, understanding the culture, and building a local network.

2. **Taxes:** Once you become a tax resident (generally if you live in Portugal for more than 183 days in a 12-month period), you will be subject to Portuguese taxes on your worldwide income. You may also be eligible for the Non-Habitual Resident (NHR) regime, which offers certain tax advantages for a period of ten years.

3. **Healthcare:** As a long-term resident, you will have access to Portugal's national healthcare service. You will need to register with a local health center and obtain a health card.

4. **Driving License:** If you are an EU citizen, you can use your home country driving license. If you are from outside the EU, you can use your international driving

license for the first six months, after which you need to exchange it for a Portuguese license.

Keep in mind, regulations can change, and requirements may vary depending on your circumstances, so it's always advisable to check with official sources or seek professional advice when planning for long-term stays in Portugal.

4.4 Requirements for Permanent Residency and Citizenship in Portugal

If you've chosen to make Portugal your long-term home, you might consider obtaining permanent residency or even citizenship. Here are the general requirements for both:

Permanent Residency:

After five years of holding a temporary residence permit, you can apply for a permanent residence permit in Portugal. To do this, you generally need to meet the following requirements:

1. **Continuous Residence:** You must have lived in Portugal for five continuous years with a valid temporary residence permit.

2. **Sufficient Means of Subsistence:** You must demonstrate that you have enough income to support yourself. The exact amount depends on the current minimum wage in Portugal.

3. **Accommodation:** You need to have a place to live, which can be proven through property deeds or a rental contract.

4. **Clean Criminal Record:** Your record should be clean in Portugal and the countries where you've lived during the last five years.

5. **Basic Portuguese Language Proficiency:** You must have basic knowledge of Portuguese, equivalent to level A2. This needs to be certified by a recognized language institution.

Portuguese Citizenship:

After six years of legal residence in Portugal, you can apply for Portuguese citizenship. Here are the standard requirements:

1. **Legal and Continuous Residence:** You must have lived legally and continuously in Portugal for six years.

2. **Sufficient Knowledge of Portuguese:** You must demonstrate sufficient knowledge of the Portuguese language, typically to the B1 level.

3. **Clean Criminal Record:** Like permanent residency, your record should be clean in Portugal and in the countries where you've lived during the last six years.

4. **Evidence of Effective Links to the Portuguese Community:** This is subjective and can include factors such as the length of residence, having a job, owning property, being involved in community organizations, or having Portuguese family members.

Remember, these requirements can be subject to change, and there might be exceptions or additional requirements for certain individuals. Therefore, it's always a good idea to consult the latest information from official Portuguese sources or a legal professional specializing in immigration.

4.5 Legal Rights and Responsibilities in Portugal

As an expat living in Portugal, understanding your legal rights and responsibilities is crucial to navigate daily life and avoid legal issues. Here's a brief overview:

Legal Rights:

1. **Equality Before the Law:** Regardless of your nationality, you have the right to be treated equally before the law. This means that you can't be discriminated against based on your race, gender, religion, nationality, or any other factor.

2. **Freedom of Speech and Expression:** Portugal guarantees the right to freedom of speech and expression, though these rights must be exercised with respect to the country's laws.

3. **Right to Privacy:** Portuguese law protects your privacy. This includes the protection of personal data, confidentiality of correspondence, and inviolability of the home.

4. **Access to Legal Representation:** If you're accused of a crime, you have the right to legal representation. If you can't afford a lawyer, the state will provide one.

5. **Access to Health Care:** Everyone residing in Portugal, including expats, has the right to access the National Health Service.

Legal Responsibilities:

1. **Obey the Law:** As an expat, you're expected to obey all Portuguese laws, even if they're different from those in your home country.

2. **Registration and Residency:** If you're staying in Portugal for more than three months, you must register with the local city council and apply for a residence permit.

3. **Taxes:** If you're residing in Portugal for more than 183 days per year, you're considered a tax resident and must pay Portuguese taxes on your worldwide income.

4. **Health Insurance:** While Portugal has universal health care, expats are generally expected to have some form of health insurance, at least until they're registered with the Portuguese Social Security system.

5. **Driving License:** Depending on your nationality, you might need to exchange your driving license for a Portuguese one after a certain period.

6. **Reporting Changes:** You must notify the Immigration and Borders Service (SEF) if there are changes to your situation, such as a new address, change of marital status, or change of job.

7. **Preservation of Public Spaces:** Portugal has strict laws regarding littering, noise, and damaging public property.

As an expat, understanding these rights and responsibilities is key to living peacefully in Portugal. It's a good idea to familiarize yourself with the local laws or consult with a legal professional to ensure that you fully understand them.

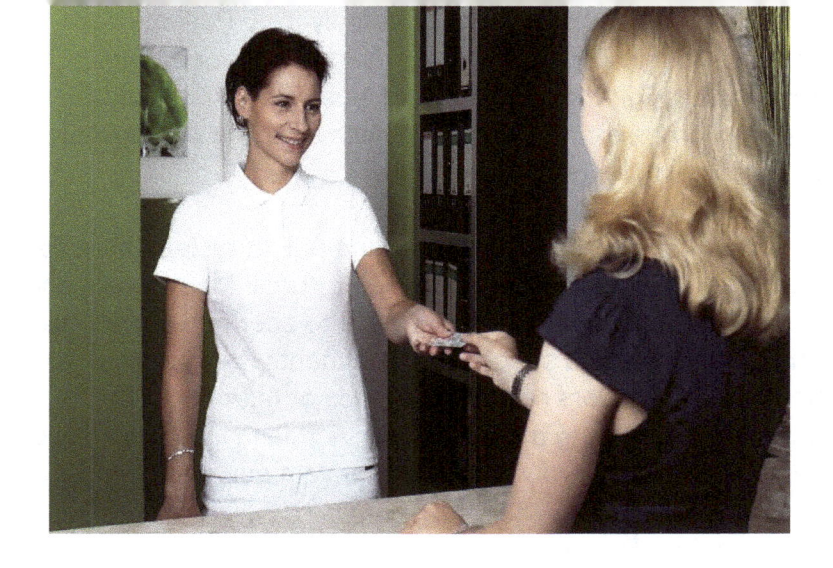

5. Health and Insurance

5.1 Healthcare System in Portugal

Portugal boasts a high-quality healthcare system, ranked among the top 15 in Europe by the World Health Organization (WHO). The system is a mix of public and private healthcare services, both providing excellent care standards.

Public Healthcare: The Portuguese National Health Service (Serviço Nacional de Saúde, SNS) provides universal healthcare coverage. It is funded through general taxation, and residents of Portugal (including expats who are legal residents) have access to it. The SNS offers a broad range of services, from general practitioner visits and hospital care to maternity services and emergency treatment. However, it's worth noting that the SNS is not entirely free. Patients need to pay user fees known as "taxas moderadoras" for certain services, though these fees are generally low. In addition, prescription medicines also come with a patient contribution, depending on the type of medication.

Private Healthcare: In addition to the public system, there is a thriving private healthcare sector in Portugal. Many locals and expats choose private healthcare due to shorter waiting times and wider access to specialized treatments. Most private healthcare providers require insurance or out-of-pocket payments, so having a comprehensive health insurance policy can be beneficial if you plan to use private services.

Pharmacies: Pharmacies are widely available across Portugal, with a distinction between "farmácias" (can sell all medicines, including prescription drugs) and "parafarmácias" (sell over-the-counter drugs and health products). Many drugs that are prescription-only in other countries can be purchased directly from a pharmacy in Portugal.

Healthcare for Expats: As an expat, your access to healthcare in Portugal depends on your residency status and where you're from. EU/EEA/Swiss citizens can use their European Health Insurance Card (EHIC) for necessary medical treatment in Portugal. Non-EU citizens should have private health insurance to cover any healthcare costs, at least until they become residents and gain access to the SNS. Regardless of whether you choose public or private healthcare, Portugal's healthcare system is well-regarded, providing high-quality care with a wide range of services.

5.2 Health Insurance Options in Portugal

Ensuring you have adequate health insurance coverage is an essential step for any expat. In Portugal, there are several health insurance options available, each with its own advantages and considerations. Here's a rundown of the options:

Portuguese National Health Service (SNS): Once you become a legal resident of Portugal, you are eligible to access the public healthcare system. Although the SNS provides a wide range of services, it's not entirely free. There are nominal patient fees for certain services and for prescription medications and wait times can be longer compared to private healthcare. However, it provides an essential safety net for all residents.

Private Health Insurance: Many expats and locals alike choose to supplement the public health system with private health insurance. Private insurance can provide more comprehensive coverage, quicker access to specialists, private hospital rooms, and often coverage for dental and optical care. There are numerous private insurance providers in Portugal, so it's advisable to shop around and find a policy that suits your healthcare needs and budget.

International Health Insurance: For those who travel frequently or split their time between countries, an international health insurance policy might be the best fit. These policies can provide coverage no matter where you are in the world, though they tend to be more expensive than local private health insurance.

European Health Insurance Card (EHIC): For EU/EEA/Swiss citizens, the EHIC provides coverage for necessary healthcare when visiting Portugal. However, it's not a replacement for comprehensive health insurance as it doesn't cover all healthcare costs or non-emergency treatments.

Travel Insurance: If you're in Portugal for a short period, travel insurance with medical coverage can provide a safety net. However, travel insurance is typically only suitable for emergency treatment and short-term stays.

When choosing health insurance in Portugal, it's important to consider your personal health needs, budget, and how often you travel. It's also worth noting that some visas and residency permits require proof of adequate health insurance as part of the application process. Always read the terms and conditions of any insurance policy carefully to ensure it provides the coverage you need.

5.3 Vaccinations and Preventive Care in Portugal

Portugal has an excellent healthcare system, and preventative care, including vaccinations, plays a significant role in maintaining public health.

Routine Vaccinations:
Portugal follows a national immunization program (Programa Nacional de Vacinação), which covers all the standard vaccines for infants, children, and adults, such as diphtheria, tetanus, polio, measles, mumps, rubella, and hepatitis B, among others. These vaccines are typically given during childhood and adolescence at specific intervals.

Travel Vaccinations:
For travelers and expats coming to Portugal, no specific vaccinations are required. However, it's always a good idea to be up to date with routine immunizations. Depending on your previous country of residence or travel history, additional vaccines might be recommended. Always consult with a healthcare professional before moving.

Flu Vaccine:
Annual flu vaccinations are recommended, especially for high-risk groups like seniors, pregnant women, and people with chronic illnesses. The flu vaccine is usually available from October through the end of the flu season, which typically lasts until spring.

Preventive Care:
Preventive care services, including regular check-ups, screenings for common diseases, and health education, are a part of the Portuguese healthcare system. Both public and private healthcare providers emphasize the importance of early detection and prevention in managing health.

To keep abreast of your vaccinations and preventive care, it's recommended to have a regular healthcare provider in Portugal. This could be a general practitioner (GP) in the public health system or a doctor in the private sector. Your healthcare provider will guide you on the vaccinations and preventive measures best suited to your personal health situation.

5.4 Dealing with Medical Emergencies in Portugal

In case of a medical emergency in Portugal, it's essential to know what to do and where to go. Here's a quick overview:

Emergency Numbers:

1. For any serious emergency, call the European emergency number 112. This number is toll-free and can be dialed from any phone, including mobile phones, even without a SIM card. Operators speak multiple languages, including English.

2. For health-related queries that are not emergencies, call SNS 24 line at 808 24 24 24. This line is staffed by healthcare professionals who can provide medical advice and direct you to the most suitable healthcare facility.

Hospital Emergencies:
Portugal has a network of public and private hospitals that provide emergency care. Large public hospitals usually have a 24-hour emergency department (pronto socorro). Keep in mind that while public healthcare is generally inexpensive, a nominal fee might be charged for emergency services.

Pharmacies:
Portuguese pharmacies (farmácias) can also help in non-emergency situations. Pharmacists are well-qualified and can provide advice on minor illnesses and injuries and recommend over-the-counter treatments. Some pharmacies are open 24 hours.

Ambulance Services:

Ambulance services are available throughout Portugal. In a serious emergency, call 112 for immediate medical assistance. However, be aware that while ambulance services are generally prompt and well-equipped, in rural areas, response times might be longer.

Private Medical Assistance:
For those with private health insurance, many insurance providers offer a 24-hour helpline. These lines can provide advice and direct you to a suitable private healthcare provider.

European Health Insurance Card (EHIC):
EU/EEA/Swiss citizens should always have their European Health Insurance Card (EHIC) handy. This card ensures you get the necessary healthcare in an emergency under the same conditions as Portuguese citizens.

In any emergency, it's essential to have your identification, contact details of next of kin, insurance details if applicable, and any important medical information (allergies, chronic conditions, medications, etc.) readily available. It's also helpful to learn some basic Portuguese medical terms or have a translation app handy if you're not fluent in the language.

5.5 Mental Health Resources in Portugal

Mental health is a vital aspect of overall well-being. Portugal offers various resources for mental health support, making it easier for expats to access the help they might need.

Public Healthcare System:

The Portuguese National Health Service (SNS) provides mental health services as part of its comprehensive healthcare offerings. These services include psychiatry, psychology, and other related fields, with care available in both outpatient and inpatient settings. However, be aware that waiting times for public mental health services can sometimes be long, particularly for non-emergency care.

Private Healthcare:
Private healthcare providers also offer mental health services, including therapy and counseling. These providers tend to have shorter waiting times and often have professionals who speak English or other foreign languages. However, costs can be higher, so having private health insurance that covers mental health care is beneficial.

Online Resources:
Online therapy and counseling have gained popularity and acceptance, offering an alternative for those who prefer remote services or who live in more rural areas. Several international platforms offer online counseling services in various languages, including English.

Support Groups:
There are several support groups, both in-person and online, for various mental health conditions. These groups can provide a community of individuals who understand your experiences, offering a platform to share and learn from others in similar situations.

Helplines:
For immediate support, there are various helplines available, such as:

1. Telefone da Amizade: A Portuguese emotional support helpline available 24/7. Call 808 237 327 (landline) or 210 027 159 (mobile).
2. SOS Voz Amiga: Offers emotional support for those in crisis or contemplating suicide. Available from 4 PM to 12 AM daily. Call 213 544 545, 912 802 669, or 963 524 660.

Mental health should never be neglected, and it's important to seek help if you're experiencing mental health difficulties. Living abroad can sometimes contribute to feelings of isolation or stress, so taking advantage of the available resources is an essential part of maintaining your mental health while in Portugal.

6. Housing and Accommodation

6.1 Renting vs. Buying in Portugal

When deciding to move to Portugal, one of the first choices you'll need to make is whether to rent or buy a property. Both options come with their own benefits and considerations, and the right choice depends on your individual circumstances, finances, and long-term plans.

Renting:

Renting a property in Portugal offers flexibility, which can be particularly beneficial for new expats who are still exploring different regions or those on temporary assignments. Rental contracts generally range from 6 months to several years, and the cost can vary significantly based on location, size, and condition of the property.

1. **Short-term rentals** are abundant in Portugal, particularly in tourist areas and cities. They can be an excellent choice for those looking to stay temporarily or while searching for long-term accommodation.

2. **Long-term rentals** typically require a contract, usually for a minimum of one year. You may need to provide identification, proof of income or employment, and sometimes a guarantor.

Buying:

Buying a property is a long-term commitment but can be a smart investment, especially given Portugal's attractive real estate market. It can also provide a sense of stability and be financially beneficial in the long term.

1. **Location and Type of Property:** Prices can vary significantly depending on the region, type, and size of the property. The most expensive areas are typically Lisbon, Porto, and the Algarve region, while the countryside and smaller cities often offer more affordable options.

2. **Legal Considerations:** Purchasing property in Portugal involves legal procedures. It's advisable to hire a lawyer to guide you through the process. It's also crucial to understand the fiscal implications of owning

property in Portugal, including property taxes and, if applicable, rental income taxes.

3. **Financing:** Several Portuguese and international banks offer mortgage loans to foreigners. Terms can vary, and eligibility often depends on your financial situation, including income, credit history, and the property's price.

In both cases, it's advisable to work with a reputable real estate agent. They can help you find suitable properties, negotiate prices, and navigate the legal requirements of renting or buying in Portugal. Whether you decide to rent or buy, ensure to carefully consider your options, take your time to decide, and seek legal advice when needed.

6.2 Typical Housing Costs in Portugal

Portugal offers a diverse real estate market, with housing costs varying greatly depending on location, type of property, and whether you're renting or buying. Here is a brief overview of the typical housing costs you can expect:

Renting:

1. **Lisbon and Porto:** As Portugal's largest cities, these areas are the most expensive. A one-bedroom city-center apartment typically costs between €800 to €1200 per month, while the same property outside the city center might range from €600 to €800.

2. **Algarve Region:** Known for its beautiful beaches and high expat population, Algarve also has higher rental

prices, though generally less than Lisbon and Porto. A one-bedroom city-center apartment might cost between €600 and €900.

3. **Smaller Cities and Rural Areas:** If you're willing to live outside the major cities or popular tourist areas, you can find much cheaper rent. In smaller cities or towns, a one-bedroom city-center apartment might cost between €300 and €500 per month.

Buying:

1. **Lisbon and Porto:** These cities are the most expensive areas to buy property in Portugal. Average property prices can range from €3,000 to €5,000 per square meter in the city center.

2. **Algarve Region:** This popular coastal region sees property prices averaging between €2,000 and €3,500 per square meter.

3. **Smaller Cities and Rural Areas:** Outside of the popular areas, you can find more affordable properties. Average prices can be as low as €1,000 per square meter or even less in rural regions.

Remember, these are just averages and actual prices can vary greatly based on factors like the exact location, size, age, and condition of the property. Utilities and maintenance costs (for homeowners) or community charges (for renters in shared buildings) can also add significantly to the monthly costs.

Also note, as an expat, securing a mortgage may come with additional challenges like higher interest rates or additional requirements compared to local buyers. Therefore, working with a reputable real estate agent and financial advisor can be very beneficial.

6.3 Choosing a Location in Portugal

Choosing where to live in Portugal depends on various factors including lifestyle preferences, budget, work commitments, and family needs. Here are a few pointers on some popular regions and what they offer:

Lisbon:
The capital and largest city of Portugal, Lisbon, is a vibrant and cosmopolitan city filled with culture, history, and nightlife. It's well-suited for those who enjoy a bustling city life and offers numerous employment opportunities. However, it is also the most expensive city in Portugal.

Porto:
Porto, the second-largest city, is known for its charming old town, port wine, and vibrant cultural scene. While it's more affordable than Lisbon, it offers a similar urban lifestyle with plenty of amenities and job opportunities.

Algarve:
Famous for its stunning coastline and sunny weather, the Algarve region is popular with retirees and those seeking a laid-back lifestyle. It's filled with expat communities, particularly from the UK, and offers a range of outdoor activities. Housing costs can be high in popular coastal towns, but cheaper options are available inland.

Coimbra:
Home to one of the world's oldest universities, Coimbra is a lively city with a youthful atmosphere. It's a great choice for academics and students and offers a mix of urban amenities and historic charm at a lower cost than Lisbon or Porto.

Madeira and the Azores:
These island groups offer a unique lifestyle with stunning natural beauty. They're perfect for nature lovers and those seeking a slower pace of life, but job opportunities are more limited and travel to the mainland can be expensive.

Rural Portugal:
The countryside offers a peaceful, slower-paced lifestyle with a low cost of living. It's a great choice for those who love nature and tranquility, but bear in mind that amenities are more limited, and you'll likely need a car to get around.

Each location in Portugal offers its unique flavor and character. It's advisable to visit different regions before deciding, if possible. Also consider practical factors like proximity to healthcare facilities, international schools (if you have kids), transport links, and your ability to speak Portuguese as English may be less widely spoken in more rural or less touristy areas.

6.4 Utilities and Other Expenses in Portugal

Beyond the cost of rent or a mortgage, living in Portugal also involves a few additional monthly expenses. Here's a breakdown of the typical costs you can expect for utilities and other living expenses:

Utilities:

1. **Electricity:** Depending on the size of your home, the number of occupants, and your usage, electricity costs can range from €50 to €100 per month. Portugal uses more renewable energy than many countries, which can sometimes help to lower costs.

2. **Water:** The average monthly water bill for a two-bedroom apartment is around €30, but this can vary based on consumption.

3. **Gas:** If your home uses gas for heating or cooking, you can expect to pay around €15-€30 per month.

4. **Internet and TV:** A package including high-speed internet, television, and sometimes a landline phone can cost from €30 to €60 per month.

Other Living Expenses:

1. **Groceries:** Monthly grocery costs can vary significantly depending on dietary preferences, but average at around €200-€300 per person.

2. **Public Transport:** A monthly pass for public transportation in cities like Lisbon or Porto costs around €30-€40.

3. **Health Insurance:** If you opt for private health insurance, costs vary widely based on coverage, but expect to pay at least €20-€40 per month for a basic plan.

4. **Dining and Entertainment:** A meal in a mid-range restaurant cost around €15-€20 per person, and cinema tickets are about €7.

5. **Fitness:** Membership at a fitness or health club in the city center costs around €30-€50 per month.

Bear in mind, these are approximate figures and actual costs can vary based on your lifestyle, location, and personal circumstances. For homeowners, additional expenses can include property taxes, home insurance, and maintenance costs. For those renting, some utilities may be included in your rent, so it's crucial to understand your rental agreement.

6.5 Land and Property Laws for Expats in Portugal

Portugal is quite welcoming to foreign property buyers, and there are few restrictions on expats purchasing real estate. However, navigating the legal system can be complex, so it's essential to understand some of the key laws and procedures:

1. **Property Purchase Process:** Buying property in Portugal involves several steps, including obtaining a Fiscal Number (Número de Identificação Fiscal) from the local tax office, hiring a lawyer to prepare a preliminary contract (Contrato de Promessa de Compra e Venda), paying a deposit, and finally signing the deed of sale (Escritura de Compra e Venda) before a notary.

2. **Taxes:** Property buyers must pay IMT (Property Transfer Tax) and Stamp Duty. There's also an annual

property tax (IMI - Imposto Municipal sobre Imóveis) based on the property's tax value. If you rent out your property, income tax is payable on the rental income.

3. **Legal Representation:** It's advisable to hire a local lawyer who understands Portuguese property law to guide you through the purchase process, ensure the property has clear title, and check for any outstanding debts or liens.

4. **Non-Habitual Resident (NHR) Regime:** This is a special tax status available to new residents, which provides tax benefits for a period of 10 years, including a potential tax exemption on foreign income.

5. **Golden Visa:** This is a residency-by-investment program that offers a route to permanent residency and citizenship in exchange for a substantial investment in Portugal, such as buying a property worth at least €500,000.

6. **Rental Laws:** If you plan to rent out your property, you need to be aware of the laws governing tenancy agreements, including rent control laws, rights and responsibilities of landlords and tenants, and tax obligations.

7. **Inheritance Laws:** Portugal has forced heirship laws, which means that a portion of your estate must go to certain relatives (like children or spouses). If you plan to leave property to someone else, you'll need to discuss this with a lawyer.

Property laws can change, and regional variations may exist. Therefore, while this guide provides a general overview, it's essential to seek professional legal advice when buying property in Portugal.

7. Cost of Living

7.1 Typical Monthly Expenses in Portugal

Understanding the typical monthly expenses is essential for any expat planning to move to a new country. In Portugal, the cost of living is relatively lower compared to many other Western European nations. Here is a rough estimate of monthly expenses you can expect:

1. **Housing:** Depending on location and property size, rent for a one-bedroom city center apartment varies between €600 and €1,200. For those who own property, the monthly mortgage payment will depend on the property's price and your loan terms.

2. **Utilities:** On average, for a two-bedroom apartment, utilities including electricity, water, heating, cooling, and garbage, can cost between €100 and €150 per month.

3. **Internet:** A broadband internet connection typically costs around €30 to €40 per month.

4. **Mobile Phone:** A basic mobile phone package with some data can cost as little as €10 to €20 per month.

5. **Transportation:** Public transportation passes for city buses, trams, and metros range from €30 to €40 per month. If you own a car, you'll need to account for fuel, insurance, and maintenance costs.

6. **Groceries:** Depending on your diet, expect to spend about €200 to €300 per month on groceries.

7. **Health Insurance:** Private health insurance plans can range greatly based on coverage, but a basic plan typically costs between €20 and €40 per month.

8. **Fitness Club:** Membership at a fitness or health club costs around €30 to €50 per month.

9. **Entertainment:** This can vary significantly depending on lifestyle but eating out at a mid-range restaurant cost about €15 to €20 per person, and a cinema ticket is about €7.

10. **Miscellaneous:** Don't forget to budget for clothing, personal care items, household goods, and any hobbies or personal activities you enjoy.

These are approximate figures and will vary based on your lifestyle, family size, and the specific city or region where you live. It's a good idea to track your spending for the first few months after you move to get a clearer picture of your personal cost of living.

7.2 Cost of Food and Groceries in Portugal

In Portugal, the cost of food and groceries is relatively reasonable compared to other Western European countries. However, the exact amount you'll spend on groceries can vary depending on your dietary habits and preferences. Here are some examples of the typical costs for various common food items:

1. **Bread:** A loaf of fresh white bread costs around €1 to €1.50.

2. **Milk:** A liter of whole fat milk is about €0.60 to €0.80.

3. **Eggs:** A dozen eggs can cost around €2 to €2.50.

4. **Cheese:** A kilogram of local cheese is around €7 to €10.

5. **Chicken:** A kilogram of boneless, skinless chicken breasts is about €5 to €7.

6. **Fruits & Vegetables:** A kilogram of apples, bananas, or oranges is usually under €2, while a head of lettuce is about €1, and a kilogram of tomatoes is around €1.50 to €2.

7. **Rice:** A kilogram of white rice is around €1.

8. **Water:** A 1.5-liter bottle of water costs less than €1.

9. **Wine:** Portugal is famous for its wine. You can get a decent bottle of local wine for €4 to €6, though prices can go much higher for premium wines.

Eating out in Portugal is also quite affordable. A meal at an inexpensive restaurant might cost €7 to €10, while a three-course meal for two at a mid-range restaurant could be around €30 to €40. A cappuccino in a café usually costs about €1.50.

Remember, prices can vary depending on the city or region and the specific shop or market where you buy your groceries. Shopping at local markets and buying seasonal produce can help to keep costs down. Also, Portugal's cuisine is rich in seafood, which is usually fresh and reasonably priced, especially near coastal areas.

7.3 Cost of Transportation in Portugal

Portugal offers a range of transportation options to suit different needs and preferences, each with its own associated costs. Here's a general breakdown:

Public Transportation:

1. **Buses and Trams:** In cities like Lisbon and Porto, a single bus or tram ticket bought onboard costs around €2, while pre-purchased tickets are cheaper at €1.50.

2. **Metro:** In Lisbon, a single metro ticket costs €1.50, and in Porto, prices start from €1.20.

3. **Monthly Passes:** A monthly public transportation pass costs about €30-€40.

Private Transportation:

1. **Car Purchase:** The price of a new car depends largely on the make and model. On average, a new compact car costs about €20,000.

2. **Car Running Costs:** Petrol costs around €1.60 per litre. The annual car insurance can vary greatly depending on factors like the vehicle's age and driver's history, but you can expect to pay around €250-€500.
3. **Taxis and Rideshares:** Taxis start at €3.25 and then charge around €0.50 per km. Rideshare apps like Uber and Bolt are also available, often at lower prices than traditional taxis.

Bicycles:

1. **Purchase:** A basic new bicycle can cost between €200-€500.

2. **Rentals:** Many cities have bike-sharing programs. In Lisbon, a yearly pass for the city bikes costs €25.

Trains:

1. **Intercity Trains:** Portugal has an extensive rail network. A second-class ticket for the 3-hour trip between Lisbon and Porto on the fast train costs around €30.

Remember, transportation costs can vary depending on your specific circumstances and usage. For instance, if you live in the city center and mainly use public transportation, your transportation costs may be lower than if you live in a suburban area and maintain a car.

7.4 Leisure and Entertainment Costs in Portugal

Costs associated with leisure and entertainment can greatly vary depending on personal preferences and lifestyle, but here's a general idea of what you might expect to pay in Portugal:

1. **Eating Out:** A meal in an inexpensive restaurant is about €10, while a three-course meal for two at a mid-range restaurant is typically between €30-€40. If you fancy a drink, domestic beer costs around €2 in a restaurant, while a glass of wine can cost anywhere from €2 to €5.

2. **Cinema:** A cinema ticket for a new release costs around €7. Some cinemas offer discounts on certain days or for specific groups like students or seniors.

3. **Gyms:** Membership at a fitness or health club costs around €30-€50 per month. Many clubs offer discounted annual memberships.

4. **Nightlife:** A cocktail drink in a club may cost between €5-€10, and a pint of beer is typically around €3.

5. **Museums and Cultural Sites:** Entry to many museums and cultural sites is around €5-€10. Some places offer free entry on certain days or times.

6. **Outdoor Activities:** Portugal is known for its beaches, hiking trails, and golf courses. Beach access is typically free, but equipment rentals like sun loungers or surfboards may cost extra. Golf green fees vary widely from €30 to over €100 depending on the course.

7. **Festivals:** Portugal hosts many festivals throughout the year. Prices vary greatly, but tickets for large music festivals typically start around €50 for a day pass.

8. **Football Matches:** Portugal is passionate about football. Ticket prices vary greatly depending on the match and seating location but can range from €15 to over €100 for premium seats at high-profile games.

Remember that your leisure and entertainment costs will depend heavily on your lifestyle and preferences. You can keep costs down by taking advantage of free or low-cost activities, such as enjoying Portugal's beautiful parks and beaches, or by taking part in local community events.

7.5 Tax Considerations in Portugal

Understanding the tax system in your new home country is crucial. In Portugal, residents are taxed on their worldwide income, while non-residents are taxed only on their Portuguese-sourced income. Here are key points you should consider:

1. **Income Tax:** The personal income tax (IRS) in Portugal operates on a progressive scale, ranging from 14.5% for incomes up to €7,112, to 48% for incomes over €80,000.

2. **Non-Habitual Residency (NHR) Regime:** Portugal offers a beneficial tax regime for new residents called the Non-Habitual Residency (NHR) program. Under this program, certain types of qualifying income are exempt from Portuguese income tax, including foreign source pensions, dividends, royalties and interest from non-Portuguese sources.

3. **VAT:** The standard VAT (Value Added Tax) rate in Portugal is 23%, though reduced rates of 13% and 6% apply to certain goods and services, such as food, books, and public transport.

4. **Social Security Contributions:** If you're employed, social security contributions are usually deducted directly from your salary. The standard rate is 11% for employees and 23.75% for employers. If you're self-employed, you'll have to make social security contributions based on your income, usually around 21.4%.

5. **Property Taxes:** Property owners need to pay an annual Municipal Property Tax (IMI), ranging from 0.3% to 0.45% of the property's tax value. When buying a property, a Property Transfer Tax (IMT) is also due, which is calculated based on the property's value, location and type, with rates up to 6.5% for urban properties.

6. **Inheritance Tax:** Portugal doesn't have inheritance tax, but a 10% stamp duty applies to Portuguese assets inherited by non-spouses or direct relatives.

7. **Wealth Tax:** There's no wealth tax in Portugal.

Taxation can be complex and often depends on your personal circumstances. Therefore, it's recommended to seek advice from a tax advisor or accountant who is familiar with the Portuguese tax system, especially if you have income from outside Portugal. Always ensure you comply with tax obligations in both your home country and Portugal.

8. Education

8.1 Overview of the Education System in Portugal

Portugal's education system is organized into three main stages: basic education, secondary education, and higher education.

1. **Basic Education:** This compulsory stage lasts for nine years and is divided into three cycles. The first cycle is from ages 6 to 10 (grades 1 to 4), the second from ages 10 to 12 (grades 5 and 6), and the third from ages 12 to 15 (grades 7 to 9). These grades are typically offered at a single school, although some larger urban

areas may have separate primary and middle schools.

2. **Secondary Education:** This stage lasts for three years, from ages 15 to 18 (grades 10 to 12). It is optional and includes general courses suitable for students planning to go to university, and vocational courses for those intending to enter the workforce after graduation.

3. **Higher Education:** This includes universities and polytechnics. Universities offer a wide range of courses in diverse fields and conduct scientific research. They grant bachelor's (3 years), master's (2 years), and doctoral degrees (3-4 years). Polytechnics offer vocational and technical courses, focusing more on practical training, and mainly grant bachelor's and master's degrees.

Aside from public schools, there are also private schools and international schools available at all stages of education. These institutions may follow a different curriculum, such as the International Baccalaureate or a curriculum from another country (like the British or American curriculum).

Education in public schools is free (though there may be some fees for materials and activities), while private and international schools charge tuition fees that can vary greatly depending on the institution.

The language of instruction in public schools is Portuguese. Therefore, children who are not fluent in Portuguese may need additional language support. This is something to consider when choosing a school, as not all public schools provide language support services for foreign students.

8.2 International and Local Schools in Portugal

In Portugal, expats have the choice of enrolling their children in local public schools, private schools, or international schools. The choice largely depends on the family's long-term plans and the child's linguistic ability and adaptability.

Local Schools:
Local public schools are free, and they provide a good opportunity for children to learn Portuguese and integrate into the local culture. The education standard in public schools is generally good, though this can vary depending on the specific area. Classes are taught in Portuguese, and while some schools do offer Portuguese as a Second Language (PSL) programs, this is not universally available.

There are also private Portuguese schools which offer a higher teacher-student ratio and often have better resources and facilities. These schools charge tuition but are generally less expensive than international schools.

International Schools:
International schools are a popular choice for expats in Portugal, especially those on shorter-term assignments or those who prefer their children to continue with a curriculum from their home country. These schools offer various international curriculums such as the International Baccalaureate (IB), British (IGCSE and A-levels), American (AP), among others.

There are several well-established international schools in Portugal, especially in and around Lisbon and Porto, as well as in the Algarve. These schools generally have a high standard of education, offer a wide range of extracurricular activities, and provide support for students who are new to the country.

However, international schools can be quite expensive, with fees varying significantly depending on the school and the age of the child. Many international schools also have long waiting lists, so it's a good idea to apply well in advance.

Remember, each child is unique, and what works well for one family might not work as well for another. Consider your child's personality, language proficiency, educational needs, and your family's long-term plans when choosing between local and international schools.

8.3 Schooling Options for Expat Children in Portugal

As an expat in Portugal, there are several schooling options for your children depending on their age, language abilities, and your personal preferences. Here's a closer look at some of the options available:

1. **Public Schools:** These schools provide free education from pre-primary to secondary level and follow the Portuguese curriculum. If your child speaks Portuguese or is young enough to pick up the language quickly, this could be a good opportunity to fully integrate into the local culture.

2. **Private Portuguese Schools:** These schools follow the Portuguese curriculum but often have smaller class sizes, better resources, and more extracurricular

activities. Tuition fees vary, but they are generally less expensive than international schools. This could be a suitable option if you plan to stay in Portugal long-term but prefer a school with more resources or a more individualized approach to education.

3. **International Schools:** These schools often follow an international curriculum such as the International Baccalaureate, the British curriculum, or the American curriculum, and classes are typically taught in English or in the school's respective language. International schools are a popular choice for families who are in Portugal for a shorter time or who prefer their children to continue with a familiar curriculum.

4. **Home Schooling:** Home schooling is legal in Portugal, and it can be an option for families who prefer a more flexible or individualized approach to education. However, it's important to follow the necessary procedures to register for home schooling and ensure the education provided meets the required standards.

5. **Bilingual Schools:** There are some schools in Portugal that offer a bilingual education, with classes taught in both Portuguese and another language (often English). These schools can provide a good middle ground for families who want their children to become fluent in Portuguese but also maintain their skills in their native language.

When choosing a schooling option for your child, consider factors such as the curriculum, language of instruction, class sizes, school culture, facilities, location, and cost. You should also consider your child's individual needs, abilities, and interests, as well as your family's long-term plans. It can be helpful to visit several schools and ask questions to get a sense of what each school offers, and which might be the best fit for your child.

8.4 Adult and Continuing Education Opportunities in Portugal

For adults and those interested in furthering their education or professional skills, Portugal offers a variety of opportunities for learning and development. Here are a few options:

1. **Universities and Polytechnics:** Portugal's higher education institutions offer a wide range of bachelor's, master's, and doctoral programs in different fields. Non-degree programs and individual courses are also available for those interested in learning a new subject without pursuing a full degree.

2. **Language Schools:** Language learning is one of the most common forms of adult education in Portugal. There are many language schools offering courses in Portuguese for foreigners, as well as other languages such as English, Spanish, French, and German. These courses can be taken at various levels, from beginner to advanced.

3. **Professional and Vocational Training:** Several institutions and organizations offer professional and vocational training courses in fields such as IT, business, marketing, hospitality, health care, and many others. These courses can be a good way to acquire

new skills or certifications for career advancement.

4. **Online Learning:** Online learning platforms like Coursera, Udemy, LinkedIn Learning, and others, allow you to take courses from anywhere in the world. You can find courses in a wide variety of subjects, from data science to art history. Many universities also offer online courses and degree programs.

5. **Community Education:** Local community centers often offer courses in a variety of areas such as arts and crafts, cooking, yoga, and more. These classes can be a good way to learn a new hobby and meet people in your local community.

6. **University of the Third Age (U3A):** For retirees and seniors, the University of the Third Age offers educational and cultural programs designed specifically for older adults. The U3A provides opportunities for learning, personal growth, and social interaction.

Before choosing a course or program, make sure to research the institution and the qualifications they offer. It's also a good idea to think about your personal interests, career goals, and how the course can benefit you in the long term.

8.5 Learning Languages in Portugal

Being an expat in a new country often requires learning a new language or improving proficiency in it. In Portugal, language learning is facilitated through various formal and informal settings:

1. **Portuguese Language Schools:** Numerous language schools in Portugal offer courses in Portuguese as a second language for all levels. These schools provide flexible schedules with options for group classes, private lessons, intensive courses, and even online learning.

2. **Tandem Learning:** Tandem learning partners people who want to learn each other's language. For example, a Portuguese person wanting to learn English might partner with an English speaker looking to learn Portuguese. This can be a free and effective way to improve your language skills while also making new friends.

3. **Language Exchanges or Conversation Groups:** In cities and larger towns, there are often language exchange groups where people meet regularly to practice different languages. These groups can be found on websites or apps like Meetup, Tandem, or even Facebook.

4. **Online Learning Platforms:** Websites and apps such as Duolingo, Babbel, Rosetta Stone, and others offer Portuguese language courses that can be accessed anytime and anywhere. These platforms typically include interactive lessons, quizzes, and practice exercises.

5. **Universities and Community Colleges:** Some universities and community colleges offer Portuguese language courses for adults. These tend to be more formal and structured, often leading to a certification.

6. **Private Tutors:** For a more personalized learning experience, you might consider hiring a private tutor. This can be particularly useful if you have specific language learning goals or need flexibility in scheduling.

Remember that language learning is a journey that takes time and practice. Immersing yourself in the language by using it in daily life, listening to Portuguese music, watching Portuguese films, and reading in Portuguese can greatly enhance your learning experience.

9. Work and Business

9.1 Employment Opportunities and Job Market Overview in Portugal

Portugal's job market offers a range of opportunities for expats, though the nature and abundance of these opportunities can vary based on your skills, qualifications, and language proficiency. Here is a brief overview of the employment landscape in Portugal:

Job Market Overview:
The Portuguese job market has seen steady growth in recent years, with low unemployment rates compared to the rest of Europe. The economy is diverse, with a mix of traditional industries and emerging sectors.

Key Industries:
Key industries in Portugal include manufacturing, automotive, energy, technology, and services. The country is also known for its strong sectors in textiles, footwear, and cork products (Portugal produces half of the world's cork).
In recent years, Portugal has been attracting a growing number of tech startups and has become a hub for digital nomads, remote workers, and tech professionals. The tourism and hospitality industry is also a significant part of the economy, especially in regions like the Algarve, Lisbon, and Porto.

Language Requirements:
While it's possible to find jobs that don't require Portuguese proficiency, especially in the tech and tourism sectors, knowing the language can significantly broaden your job opportunities and make integrating into the workplace easier.

Job Search:
Many Portuguese companies advertise job openings on online platforms like LinkedIn, Indeed, and Glassdoor. There are also several local job search websites, including Net-Empregos and Sapo Emprego. Networking can also play a crucial role in finding job opportunities, so consider joining local business groups or attending networking events.

Work Culture:
The work culture in Portugal is somewhat relaxed compared to some other European countries, with a focus on relationships and work-life balance. However, professionalism and respect are still highly valued in the workplace.
In conclusion, the job market in Portugal offers a variety of opportunities for expats, but it's important to be proactive and adaptable in your job search. Brushing up on your Portuguese

and understanding the local work culture can also be hugely beneficial.

9.2 Professional Qualifications and Certifications in Portugal

Depending on your career field, you may need to have your professional qualifications or certifications recognized in Portugal. Here's an overview of how the process generally works:

Recognition of Foreign Qualifications:
For many professions in Portugal, especially regulated ones like medicine, law, or teaching, you'll need to have your foreign qualifications recognized. The process varies depending on the profession and often involves the relevant professional body or regulatory authority. You may be required to provide official translations of your certificates and possibly pass an equivalency exam or complete additional training.
The National Academic Recognition Information Centre (NARIC) in Portugal can provide information on the recognition of foreign academic qualifications.

Professional Development and Further Certification:
Various institutions in Portugal offer professional development courses and certifications that may be beneficial or required for certain careers. For instance, if you're in the tech sector, you might consider additional certifications in areas like data analysis or cybersecurity.

Language proficiency can also be a critical qualification in Portugal. If you plan to work in a role requiring Portuguese language skills, it could be beneficial to take a language proficiency test, such as those provided by the Camões Institute.

Understanding Your Industry's Needs:
Different industries may value certain qualifications or certifications over others. Conduct thorough research or seek advice from industry professionals to understand what's valued in your field in Portugal. LinkedIn and other professional networking sites can be helpful resources for this kind of research.

In Summary:
While the process of having your qualifications recognized in Portugal can be time-consuming, it's a necessary step for certain professions. Additionally, furthering your qualifications with Portuguese or industry-specific certifications could enhance your employability. It's important to do your research, reach out to relevant professional bodies, and prepare for this process as part of your move to Portugal.

9.3 Starting a Business in Portugal

Portugal is an attractive location for entrepreneurs due to its strategic location, access to the European market, supportive government policies, and burgeoning startup scene. Here's an overview of how to start a business in Portugal:

Business Structure:
The first step is to decide on a business structure. The most common types are Sole Trader (Empresário em Nome Individual), Limited Liability Company (Sociedade por Quotas), and Public Limited Company (Sociedade Anónima). Each has its advantages, disadvantages, and specific requirements, so

you should choose based on the nature and scale of your business.

Registration Process:
Next, you need to register your business. This involves a few steps:
1. Obtain a Portuguese Tax Number (Número de Identificação Fiscal, NIF)
2. Register a unique company name
3. Draft and sign a deed of incorporation
4. Register the business with the Commercial Register
5. Obtain a Social Security number for the company

Opening a Bank Account:
You will also need to open a bank account in Portugal for your business. The requirements vary between banks but generally include identification, tax number, and business registration documents.

Licenses and Permits:
Depending on your business's nature, you may require certain licenses or permits. For example, a restaurant would need health and safety inspections and permits, while a tour company might need specific tourism licenses.

Taxes and Accounting:
Businesses in Portugal are subject to various taxes, including Corporate Income Tax (IRC), VAT (IVA), and Social Security contributions. You'll need to register for these taxes and ensure you comply with all reporting and payment requirements. Hiring an accountant can be very helpful, especially when starting.

Support for Startups:
Portugal offers various support programs for startups, including financial incentives, coworking spaces, and networking events. Portugal's startup visa program also makes it easier for non-EU/EEA/Swiss entrepreneurs to establish their businesses in Portugal.

Starting a business in Portugal involves several legal and administrative steps, but the supportive business environment and potential access to the broader European market can make it a worthwhile endeavor. Always seek professional advice to ensure you fully understand the requirements and implications.

9.4 Labor Laws and Employee Rights in Portugal

In Portugal, labor laws aim to protect both employees and employers, outlining their respective rights and responsibilities. Here is a broad overview of the main aspects related to employee rights:

Working Hours and Overtime:
The standard workweek in Portugal is 40 hours, typically spread over five days. Overtime is usually paid at a higher rate, and there are limits on the number of overtime hours an employee can work.

Annual Leave and Public Holidays:
Employees in Portugal are entitled to 22 days of annual leave. In addition to these, there are also 13 public holidays. If a holiday falls on a weekend, it's not usually moved to a

weekday.

Minimum Wage and Compensation:
Portugal has a national minimum wage that is adjusted periodically. Other aspects of compensation, like bonuses or commissions, are typically outlined in the employment contract.

Termination and Severance Pay:
Employment contracts can be terminated by either the employee or employer, usually with notice. In some cases, severance pay may be required, especially if the termination is initiated by the employer.

Discrimination and Harassment:
Portuguese labor laws protect workers from discrimination based on factors like gender, race, age, disability, religious beliefs, and sexual orientation. Harassment, including sexual harassment, is also illegal.

Maternity and Paternity Leave:
Portugal has provisions for both maternity and paternity leave. Mothers are entitled to an initial maternity leave of 120 or 150 days, depending on how the days are divided before and after birth. Fathers are mandated to take at least five days of leave during the first month following birth.

Health and Safety:
Employers are required to provide a safe and healthy work environment. This includes following safety regulations, providing necessary protective equipment, and taking steps to prevent workplace accidents and illnesses.
It's essential for both employees and employers to familiarize themselves with Portuguese labor laws to understand their

9.5 Income Tax Considerations in Portugal

Understanding your income tax obligations is a crucial part of living and working in Portugal. Here's a general overview of the income tax system:

Tax Residency:
You are considered a tax resident in Portugal if you spend more than 183 days in the country within a tax year, or if you have a house in Portugal that can be occupied at any time during the year. Tax residents are taxed on their worldwide income. Non-residents are taxed only on their Portugal-sourced income.

Income Tax Rates:
Portugal uses a progressive income tax system, where the tax rate increases as your income does. The rates range from 14.5% for income up to €7,112, to 48% for income over €80,882.

Tax Year and Returns:
The tax year in Portugal is the calendar year, and income tax returns should be filed between April 1 and June 30 of the following year.

Non-Habitual Resident (NHR) Scheme:
Portugal offers a Non-Habitual Resident scheme, which allows certain professionals to pay a reduced rate of tax on their income for the first ten years they live in the country. The program applies to high value-added professions, like

scientists, artists, and IT professionals, as well as pensioners receiving foreign pensions.

Double Taxation Agreements:
Portugal has double taxation agreements with several countries to prevent individuals from being taxed on the same income in two countries. If you're from a country that has such an agreement with Portugal, you may be able to claim tax relief.

Freelancers and Self-Employed Workers:
Freelancers and self-employed workers must make Social Security contributions and may need to charge VAT, depending on their profession and income. They can also deduct certain expenses from their taxable income.
Tax law can be complicated, and the information provided here is a general guide. It's strongly recommended that you consult with a tax professional or advisor to understand your personal tax situation.

9.6 Networking and Professional Groups in Portugal

Professional networking is an essential tool for success in any career. In Portugal, several networking and professional groups can help you build connections, learn about your industry, and find new opportunities. Here's an overview:

Local Networking Events:
Portugal, especially cities like Lisbon and Porto, frequently hosts networking events across various sectors. Websites like Eventbrite or Meetup can help you find relevant events. Also, keep an eye on local chambers of commerce and industry

associations for their events.

Online Professional Networks:
LinkedIn is popular in Portugal, and many professionals use it for networking, job hunting, and staying informed about their industry. You can find numerous professional groups on LinkedIn related to Portugal and your specific industry.

Expat Groups:
Expat groups can be an excellent resource for meeting people who have also moved to Portugal. These groups often organize social events and can provide advice and support for adjusting to life in Portugal. InterNations and Meetup are good platforms to find such groups.

Industry-Specific Organizations:
Depending on your profession, there may be professional associations or organizations in Portugal that you can join. These often host events, provide resources, and offer opportunities for continuing professional development.

Coworking Spaces:
Coworking spaces are popular among freelancers, remote workers, and startups in Portugal. These spaces often host networking events and can be a great place to meet people working in a variety of sectors.

Volunteering:
Volunteering can be another excellent way to meet people and contribute to your local community. Look for opportunities through local non-profit organizations, community groups, or online platforms like VolunteerMatch.
Networking in Portugal, like in many places, can be an effective way to advance your career, learn new skills, and feel

more connected to your community. Whether you prefer online or in-person networking, there are plenty of opportunities available.

10. Language and Culture

10.1 Local Languages in Portugal

The official and most widely spoken language in Portugal is Portuguese. Here's a deeper dive into the language scenario in the country:

Portuguese:
Portuguese is a Romance language that developed from Latin roots and is closely related to Spanish, Italian, and French. It is the sixth most spoken language globally, thanks to Portugal's historical role in global exploration, trade, and colonization. Portuguese in Portugal differs slightly from the variant spoken in Brazil, particularly in terms of pronunciation, some

vocabulary, and certain grammatical structures.

English Proficiency:
While Portuguese is the primary language, English is commonly understood, particularly in larger cities, tourist areas, and among younger generations. Many Portuguese people are multilingual, with English being the most popular second language due to the country's strong ties with the rest of Europe and the wider world. However, proficiency can vary, and in rural areas, English may be less widely understood.

Other Languages:
In certain areas of Portugal, other languages can be heard. These include Mirandese, spoken in the region of Miranda do Douro, which has co-official status locally. There's also a small community of Spanish speakers along the border with Spain.

As an expat in Portugal, you'll likely find English sufficient for most day-to-day tasks. However, learning Portuguese will significantly enhance your experience, help you integrate into the local culture, and may be necessary if you plan to work in a Portuguese-speaking environment. There are numerous language schools and online platforms that offer Portuguese courses, from beginner to advanced levels.

10.2 Cultural Norms and Etiquette in Portugal

Portuguese culture is warm and friendly, with a strong emphasis on family and community. When interacting with locals, you'll find a few cultural norms and etiquette rules that will guide your interactions:

Greetings:
A handshake is the most common form of greeting in a formal or first-time meeting scenario. Among friends, men usually perform a mutual pat on the back, and women kiss each other twice, starting with the right cheek. It's customary to greet every person individually when entering or leaving a group.

Titles:
Use formal titles (Senhor for Mr., Senhora for Mrs.) until invited to use first names. Professional titles, such as Doctor or Professor, are used frequently.

Hospitality:
The Portuguese are known for their hospitality. If invited to a Portuguese home, it is customary to bring a small gift, such as flowers, chocolates, or wine.

Dining Etiquette:
Always keep your hands on the table (but not your elbows) and remember to say "Bom apetite" (Enjoy your meal) before you start eating. If you're invited to a restaurant, the person who does the inviting usually pays the bill.

Punctuality:
While Portugal is a Southern European country and a more relaxed attitude towards time is often seen, punctuality is generally appreciated, especially for business meetings.

Respect for Tradition:
Portuguese people have a deep respect for tradition and history. This can be seen in the careful preservation of their historic sites and in their many festivals and customs that date back centuries.

Dress Code:
Portuguese people take pride in dressing well. In business settings, conservative and formal attire is the norm. In social settings, smart casual is usually appropriate.
Understanding these norms will not only help you feel more comfortable and avoid misunderstandings but also show your respect for the local culture, making it easier to build relationships and integrate into Portuguese life.

10.3 Holidays and Festivals in Portugal

Portugal has a rich tradition of holidays and festivals that showcase the country's history, culture, and love for celebration. Here are some notable ones:

National Holidays:
Some of Portugal's national holidays include Liberty Day (April 25th, marking the Carnation Revolution), Portugal Day (June 10th, celebrating Portugal's national poet Luís de Camões), and Restoration of Independence (December 1st, celebrating the end of Spanish rule).

Religious Festivals:
Portugal is predominantly Catholic, and religious holidays are widely celebrated. These include Easter, with its processions and traditional sweets, and Christmas, marked by Midnight Mass and family gatherings. The Feast of São João (St. John) on June 24th is a significant event, especially in Porto, featuring street parties, fireworks, and the tradition of hitting each other with soft plastic hammers.

Carnaval:
Carnaval, like Mardi Gras, is celebrated in February or early March, depending on the liturgical calendar. The largest celebration takes place in Torres Vedras, with parades, costumes, and dancing.

Fado Music Festivals:
Fado is a traditional form of Portuguese music, recognized by UNESCO as part of the world's intangible cultural heritage. Lisbon and Coimbra are known for their fado festivals, where you can enjoy soulful music.

Wine Festivals:
Given Portugal's renown as a wine-producing country, several regions host wine festivals, usually coinciding with the harvest season. Douro and Alentejo are particularly famous for these events.

Sardine Festival:
The Feast of St. Anthony (Festival de Santo António) in Lisbon is famous for its grilled sardines, a favorite Portuguese dish, and is celebrated with street parties and parades.
Living in Portugal gives you the opportunity to participate in these celebrations and learn about the local culture. Each region and even individual towns have their own unique festivals and traditions, so there's always something to explore.

10.4 Integrating into the Local Community in Portugal

Integration into the local community is an essential part of the expat experience. It helps you understand and appreciate the host country's culture, build meaningful relationships, and feel more at home. Here are some tips for integrating into the local community in Portugal:

Learning Portuguese:
While many Portuguese people speak English, especially in cities and tourist areas, learning the local language can open doors to deeper connections. It shows your commitment to understanding and respecting the local culture, and it will make everyday tasks and interactions easier.

Participating in Local Events and Festivals:
As mentioned earlier, Portugal has a rich cultural calendar. Participating in these events is an excellent way to engage with the community, learn about Portuguese traditions, and meet locals.

Joining Social and Cultural Groups:
There are many social and cultural groups that welcome international members. These may be language exchange groups, sports clubs, volunteer organizations, or groups centered around shared hobbies. This can be a great way to make local friends and expand your social network.

Understanding Cultural Norms:
Showing respect for local customs and etiquette, as well as an interest in the country's history and traditions, will go a long way towards integrating into the community. This includes everything from table manners to accepted social behaviors.

Contributing to the Community:
Whether it's volunteering, participating in local initiatives, or supporting local businesses, showing that you're invested in the well-being of the community can help forge deeper connections with locals.

Engaging with Neighbors:
Simple acts like greeting neighbors, attending neighborhood events, or even joining a neighborhood association can help you feel part of the community.

Remember, integration is a gradual process that takes time and patience. It might feel challenging at times, but the reward of feeling at home in your new country is well worth the effort.

10.5 Religion and Its Role in Portuguese Culture

Religion plays a significant role in Portuguese society and culture, with Roman Catholicism being the predominant faith. The influence of religion can be seen in various aspects of daily life and is integral to understanding the country's traditions, holidays, and customs.

Catholicism:
Most of the Portuguese population identifies as Roman Catholic, although not everyone actively practices. The country's Catholic heritage is evident in the many churches that dot the landscape, from grand cathedrals in the cities to small chapels in rural areas. Several religious festivals and holidays, such as Easter and Christmas, are widely celebrated, and processions and other religious events form an important part of local community life.

Secularization:
In recent decades, Portugal has undergone significant secularization, and there has been a rise in the number of people identifying as non-religious. The separation of church and state is enshrined in the Portuguese Constitution, ensuring religious freedom for all, and society is generally

tolerant and accepting of different faiths.

Other Religions:
While the Catholic Church dominates, other Christian denominations are present, including Protestant, Orthodox, and Jehovah's Witnesses. There's also a small but significant Muslim community, primarily consisting of immigrants from former Portuguese colonies in Africa. Other religions, such as Buddhism, Hinduism, and Judaism, have smaller followings.

Religion and Culture:
Religion has influenced Portuguese culture in many ways, from the country's rich heritage of religious art and architecture to its traditions and festivals. Even the Portuguese language contains many phrases and expressions with religious origins. Understanding the role of religion in Portuguese society can enrich your understanding of the country's culture and history, even if you do not follow a particular faith. It's also important to respect the local religious customs, such as dressing modestly when visiting places of worship and observing quiet during religious ceremonies or events.

11. Practical Information

11.1 Transportation System in Portugal

Portugal has a comprehensive and efficient transportation network that provides various options for getting around, both within cities and between different regions of the country.

Public Transportation:
In cities like Lisbon and Porto, you'll find extensive public transportation networks that include buses, trams, and metros. These systems are reliable, and they can take you to most areas within the city. Public transport is also quite affordable, with discounts available for monthly or annual passes.

Trains:
The train network in Portugal is managed by Comboios de Portugal (CP). There are regular services between major cities and towns, and the trains are generally comfortable and punctual. High-speed trains, such as the Alfa Pendular, provide rapid links between Lisbon and Porto, Faro, and Braga.

Buses:
For more remote or rural areas not served by train, intercity and regional buses are an alternative. Rede Expressos is a popular long-distance bus company with routes that cover the entire country.

Taxis and Rideshares:
Taxis are readily available in most urban areas. They can be hailed on the street, picked up at taxi ranks, or booked over the phone. In addition to traditional taxis, rideshare services like Uber and Bolt operate in larger cities.

Driving:
Portugal has a well-maintained network of roads and highways, and driving can be an efficient way to get around, especially in more rural areas. However, keep in mind that traffic in big cities can be congested, and parking can be challenging to find. If you're planning to drive, you should familiarize yourself with the local driving laws.

Biking and Walking:
In recent years, there has been a push to make Portuguese cities more pedestrian- and bike-friendly. Lisbon and Porto both have bike-sharing programs, and there are dedicated cycling lanes in many areas.

Air Travel:
Portugal has several international airports, with the largest in Lisbon (Lisbon Humberto Delgado Airport) and Porto (Francisco Sá Carneiro Airport). These provide connections to other cities in Europe and international destinations. Understanding the transportation system will not only make your day-to-day life more convenient but also open opportunities to explore different parts of the country.

11.2 Internet and Telecommunications in Portugal

Portugal boasts a well-developed and modern telecommunications infrastructure, making it easy to stay connected. Whether you're planning to work remotely, stay in touch with friends and family abroad, or simply browse the internet, understanding the local telecommunications landscape will help.

Internet:
Broadband internet is widely available throughout Portugal, including both cable and ADSL services. In major cities and towns, fiber-optic connections offer high-speed internet and are provided by companies like MEO, Vodafone, and NOS. Internet cafes are less common than in the past, but most libraries offer free Wi-Fi, and it's often available in cafes and other public spaces.

Mobile Networks:
Portugal has several mobile network providers, the largest being MEO, NOS, and Vodafone. They offer a variety of plans, including pay-as-you-go and contract options. 4G coverage is widespread, and 5G is being rolled out. You can purchase a

SIM card in various locations, including shops, supermarkets, and kiosks.

Landlines:
While landline phones are becoming less common due to the prevalence of mobile phones, they can still be found in most homes and businesses. They're often bundled with internet and television services.

Television and Radio:
Cable TV is common in Portugal and offers a wide variety of channels, both Portuguese and international. Streaming services such as Netflix and Amazon Prime are also widely available. Radio stations in Portugal offer a mix of music, news, and talk programs, with both public and private broadcasters.

Postal Services:
The national postal service in Portugal is CTT. It offers reliable mail and parcel services, as well as financial services and retail products. In addition to traditional mail, courier services such as DHL and FedEx operate in Portugal.

Overall, staying connected in Portugal is straightforward. However, it's worth comparing rates and packages from different providers to find the best deal to suit your needs.

11.3 Local Cuisine in Portugal

Portuguese cuisine is diverse and flavorful, with a rich culinary tradition influenced by the country's maritime history and various cultural influences over the centuries. From fresh seafood to hearty meat dishes, and from delicious pastries to world-renowned wines, there's a wealth of gastronomic experiences to explore.

Seafood:
Given Portugal's extensive coastline, seafood is a staple of the local cuisine. Dishes to try including "bacalhau" (salted cod), often claimed to be prepared in over a thousand different ways, "sardinhas assadas" (grilled sardines), and "caldeirada," a hearty fish stew. Shellfish, like clams and prawns, are also widely enjoyed.

Meat Dishes:
While seafood is prominent, meat dishes are also central to Portuguese cuisine. "Cozido à Portuguesa" is a traditional boiled meat dish with vegetables, while "leitão assado" (roast suckling pig) and "Alentejana" (pork with clams) showcase the country's ability to create hearty, flavorful meals.

Dairy and Sweets:
Portugal has a variety of cheeses, with "Serra da Estrela" being one of the most famous. The country is also known for its pastries, with "pastéis de nata" (egg custard tarts) being a must-try. Other desserts include "arroz doce" (rice pudding) and "bolo rei" (king's cake), a traditional Christmas treat.

Wine:
Portugal is famous for its wines. The Douro Valley and Alentejo regions produce excellent red and white wines, but it's the sweet, fortified Port wine and the unique green wine ("vinho verde") that are perhaps the most emblematic of the country.

Local Markets and Dining Out:
Local markets are a great place to explore Portugal's culinary diversity. Here, you can find everything from fresh fish and produce to locally made cheeses and cured meats. Dining out is also a popular activity, and there are options to suit all tastes and budgets, from small, family-run "tascas" to Michelin-starred restaurants.

Understanding and experiencing the local cuisine will not only make your stay in Portugal more enjoyable but will also provide insight into the country's culture and traditions.

11.4 Safety and Security Tips in Portugal

Portugal is generally a safe country, regularly ranking as one of the safest in the world. However, like anywhere, it's important to be aware of your surroundings and take common-sense precautions. Here are some tips to help you stay safe:

Personal Safety:
- Be aware of your surroundings, especially in crowded tourist areas, where pickpockets can operate. Keep your belongings secure and avoid displaying expensive jewelry or electronic devices openly.
- Avoid isolated areas after dark, particularly in larger cities. Stick to well-lit, populated areas.
- If you're traveling alone, let someone know your plans and check in regularly.

Traffic Safety:
- While Portugal's roads are generally well-maintained, driving styles can be aggressive, and accident rates are higher than in some other European countries. If

you're driving, be cautious, especially on narrow, winding country roads.
- Pedestrians should be mindful of traffic when crossing the road, even when using a pedestrian crossing. Not all drivers stop as required.

Natural Disasters and Weather:
- Portugal can experience forest fires in the hot, dry summer months, particularly in rural and woodland areas. Be aware of local warnings and avoid starting open fires.
- Coastal areas can experience strong ocean currents, so always heed local advice when swimming or participating in water sports.

Emergency Services:
- The national emergency number in Portugal is 112. This will connect you to police, fire, and medical services.

Health:
- Ensure you have appropriate travel insurance to cover any medical costs. While Portugal has a good healthcare system, treatment can be expensive for non-residents.
- Be cautious in the sun, particularly in summer. Use sunblock, seek shade during the hottest part of the day, and stay well hydrated.

Remember, most visits to Portugal are trouble-free, but staying informed and taking basic precautions can help ensure your time in this beautiful country is safe and enjoyable.

11.5 Shopping and Food in Portugal

Whether you're in need of groceries, seeking local produce, or looking for a unique memento of your time in Portugal, the country's shopping and food scene offers a range of experiences.

Groceries:
Supermarkets in Portugal are plentiful and range from larger chains such as Continente, Pingo Doce, and Intermarché to smaller local shops and convenience stores. They typically carry a wide range of goods, including fresh produce, local and imported items, household necessities, and more.

Local Markets:
For fresh local produce, bakeries, and sometimes even fish and meat, local markets or "mercados" are a great choice. They offer a taste of the region's seasonal produce and give an authentic insight into the local way of life. Some popular ones include Mercado da Ribeira in Lisbon and Mercado do Bolhão in Porto.

Specialty Foods:
Portugal is known for its specialty foods and drinks. Seek out local olive oils, cheeses, and the famous Port and Madeira wines, as well as the less well-known but equally delicious Vinho Verde and various red and white wines from regions like Douro and Alentejo.

Shopping:
From traditional ceramic tiles ("azulejos") to cork products and handmade jewelry, there are plenty of unique souvenirs and gifts to bring home. Shopping centers and high-street brands are common in larger towns and cities. For a more unique

shopping experience, check out local markets and shops, where you'll find items crafted by local artisans.

Dining Out:
Portugal offers a range of dining options, from affordable "tascas" (traditional small restaurants or taverns) serving hearty local fare to world-class gourmet restaurants. Portugal's café culture is also vibrant, and no day is complete without a coffee ("bica" in Lisbon, "cimbalino" in Porto) and a pastry, such as the famous "pastel de nata."

When shopping and dining in Portugal, it's worth noting that tipping is customary but not mandatory. A tip of 10-15% is common in restaurants, and rounding up to the nearest euro is standard in taxis or for smaller services.

11.6 Pet Ownership and Animal Laws in Portugal

Portugal is generally a pet-friendly country and it's common to see dogs in parks, on sidewalks, and in some restaurants or cafes. However, there are laws and regulations in place to ensure the welfare of animals and the safety of the public.

Pet Registration and Identification:
In Portugal, it's a legal requirement to register and microchip dogs. Registration is done at the local town hall ("Junta de Freguesia") and microchipping at a veterinarian's office. Cats do not legally require microchipping, but it is highly recommended.

Vaccination:
Pets must be vaccinated against common diseases. Dogs are required to have a rabies vaccination and it's recommended for cats as well.

Pet Passport:
For travel within the European Union, a pet passport is required, documenting all the vaccinations and treatments the pet has received. Your local vet can provide this.

Restricted Breeds:
Portugal has restrictions on certain dog breeds considered potentially dangerous. These include the Staffordshire Terrier, Rottweiler, Dogo Argentino, Fila Brasileiro, and Tosa Inu. Owners of these breeds require a special license and must adhere to specific regulations.

Animal Welfare:
Portugal has strong animal welfare laws. Abandonment is illegal and considered a crime. The law also requires owners to provide adequate living conditions, food, and veterinary care for their pets.

Public Spaces:
In general, dogs must be kept on a leash in public places. Some parks have designated off-leash areas. It's the owner's responsibility to clean up after their pets.

Housing:
While it's common for rentals to allow pets, it's not a given, and it's always best to check with the landlord beforehand.
Having a pet in Portugal can be a wonderful experience, but it's important to be aware of and comply with all the local laws and regulations. This ensures not only the welfare of your pet

but also contributes to a harmonious coexistence with others in the community.

12. Life as an Expat

12.1 Expat Communities in Portugal

Portugal is home to a thriving expat community, drawn to the country's relaxed pace of life, beautiful landscapes, friendly locals, and affordable cost of living. Many expats in Portugal are from the UK, Germany, France, the Netherlands, and increasingly from North America too. Here's a brief overview of expat communities in Portugal:

Lisbon and Porto:
These bustling cities have the largest expat communities due to their economic opportunities, cultural attractions, and cosmopolitan lifestyle. Many young professionals, digital nomads, and entrepreneurs find themselves drawn to these cities.

Algarve:
The sunny Algarve region in the south of Portugal is a favorite among retirees, particularly from the UK and other parts of Europe, due to its climate, beautiful beaches, and golf courses.

Madeira and the Azores:
These island regions are becoming increasingly popular with expats seeking a quieter, nature-focused lifestyle. They are particularly attractive to retirees, remote workers, and those involved in the tourism sector.

Connecting with Expat Communities:

1. **Online Forums and Social Media:** Websites like Internations, Expatica, Meetup, and Facebook have numerous groups dedicated to expats in Portugal. These can be great resources for asking questions, finding events, and making connections.

2. **Local Clubs and Groups:** Many towns and cities have clubs and groups where expats can connect. This could be a language exchange group, a sports club, or an international women's group, for example.

3. **Networking and Professional Events:** For those moving for work or business, networking events can be a valuable way to meet other expats in the same field. Many coworking spaces host such events.

4. **Volunteering:** Volunteering can be a rewarding way to meet people and feel part of the community. Look for local charities or community organizations in need of

help.

Remember, while it can be comforting to connect with other expats, it's also important to build relationships with locals to fully integrate and get the most out of your experience living in Portugal.

12.2 Making Local Friends in Portugal

Making local friends in Portugal can greatly enhance your expat experience, offering you insights into the culture, language, traditions, and everyday life that you might not gain from expat-only circles. Here are some suggestions on how to meet locals and build meaningful friendships:

Language Exchange:
One of the best ways to make local friends is through language exchange meetups, where locals looking to practice English or other languages meet with foreigners wanting to learn Portuguese. This is not only a great way to improve your language skills but also to form lasting friendships.

Join Local Clubs or Groups:
Whether it's a sports club, a choir, a book club, or a cooking class, joining a group where locals and expats share a common interest can pave the way for genuine friendships.

Volunteer:
Participating in local volunteering initiatives allows you to contribute to the community while meeting locals who share your altruistic interests.

Attend Local Events and Festivals:

Portugal has a rich calendar of festivals, concerts, and cultural events. Attending these not only gives you an insight into local traditions but also provides a natural setting for striking up conversations with locals.

Neighborhood Community:
Don't overlook your immediate neighborhood. Building relationships with your neighbors, frequenting local shops, and getting involved in neighborhood activities can lead to meaningful connections.

Workplace and Professional Networking:
If you're working in Portugal, your workplace is a natural environment to meet and befriend locals. Additionally, attending professional networking events can broaden your circle.

Children's School and Activities:
If you're moving with children, their school events, and extracurricular activities are perfect occasions to meet local parents.

While Portuguese people are generally friendly and welcoming, keep in mind that it might take time to form deep friendships. Portuguese people often have close-knit circles of friends from childhood or their school years. However, with time, patience, and the right approach, you can forge strong bonds with locals during your expat journey in Portugal.

12.3 Dealing with Homesickness in Portugal

Homesickness is a common challenge faced by many expats, no matter where in the world they've relocated. The excitement of new experiences can sometimes be overshadowed by the longing for the familiar - your home country, family, friends, and traditions. Here are some strategies to help cope with homesickness in Portugal:

Stay Connected with Home:
Thanks to technology, staying in touch with loved ones back home is easier than ever. Regular calls, video chats, or social media updates can help you feel more connected.

Establish Routines:
Creating new routines can help Portugal feel more like home. This can involve finding a local café to enjoy your morning coffee, a favorite running route, or a weekly market to shop for groceries.

Get Involved Locally:
The more you participate in local life, the more you'll feel part of the community. Attend neighborhood gatherings, join a local club, or volunteer for a local cause.

Learn the Language:
While many Portuguese people speak English, learning Portuguese can help you feel more at home and facilitate deeper connections with locals.

Explore Portugal:
Take time to explore your new country. Visit different cities, try new foods, learn about the history and culture. Each

exploration can lead to a new appreciation for your host country.

Seek Support:
Reach out to fellow expats who are likely to experience similar feelings. There are also professional counselors who specialize in expat adjustment and can provide helpful strategies.

Keep Mementos of Home:
Having familiar items around, like photographs or favorite books, can provide comfort.

Practice Self-Care:
Regular exercise, a healthy diet, and adequate sleep can help maintain your emotional health. Mindfulness or meditation can also be useful.

It's important to remember that homesickness is a normal part of the expat experience and often temporary. It's okay to miss home while also embracing your new life in Portugal. With time and patience, Portugal will start to feel like home too.

12.4 Benefits and Challenges Specific to Portugal

Every country comes with its unique set of benefits and challenges for expats, and Portugal is no exception. Here's a look at some specific advantages and potential hurdles you might face while living in Portugal:

Benefits:

1. **Cost of Living:** Portugal's cost of living is relatively low compared to other Western European countries, making it an attractive destination for expats.

2. **Climate:** Portugal boasts a Mediterranean climate, with hot, dry summers and mild winters, which many expats find attractive.

3. **Culture:** Portugal has a rich cultural heritage, with traditions dating back centuries. The country's history, cuisine, music (like Fado), and festivals provide a culturally enriching experience.

4. **Safety:** Portugal consistently ranks as one of the safest countries in the world, which can be a comfort for families and solo expats alike.

5. **Language:** While Portuguese is the national language, English is widely spoken, especially in tourist areas and among the younger population. This can ease the transition for English-speaking expats.

Challenges:

1. **Language:** Although English is relatively common, there are areas where Portuguese is predominantly spoken. If you're planning to live outside of the major cities, learning Portuguese can be essential.

2. **Bureaucracy:** Many expats report that dealing with bureaucratic processes can be a challenge in Portugal. The paperwork for visas, residency, setting up utilities,

or buying property can be complex and time-consuming.

3. **Employment:** While there are opportunities, particularly in sectors like IT, tourism, and teaching English, the job market can be competitive. It's important to research thoroughly if you're planning on finding employment in Portugal.

4. **Driving:** Driving in Portugal can be a bit challenging for expats, especially in congested city centers with narrow roads. Understanding Portuguese Road signs and rules will take some time.

5. **Healthcare:** While the healthcare system in Portugal is good, there may be long waiting times for non-emergency procedures. Many expats choose to have private health insurance for more immediate access to services.

Understanding these benefits and challenges can help you prepare better for your move and adapt more quickly to your new life in Portugal.

13. Planning the Move

13.1 Timeline and Checklist for Moving to Portugal

Planning a move to another country requires detailed and timely planning. Here is a suggested timeline and checklist to help ensure a smooth transition to your new life in Portugal:

6-12 Months Before Move:

1. **Research:** Begin researching about Portugal's lifestyle, cost of living, housing, and education system if you have children. Start learning Portuguese if you don't already speak it.

2. **Visa Application:** Determine the type of visa you will need and begin the application process.

3. **Health Insurance:** Research health insurance options in Portugal and what would best fit your needs.

4. **Finances:** Speak to a financial advisor about managing your finances while abroad, including tax implications.

3-6 Months Before Move:

1. **Housing:** Start looking for accommodation in Portugal. Decide whether you want to rent or buy and which city or region you prefer.

2. **Schools:** If you have children, research schooling options and apply to secure a place.

3. **Health Checks:** Schedule necessary medical, dental, and eye check-ups. Also, verify if any vaccinations are required.

4. **Driving License:** Check the requirements for driving in Portugal. You may need to apply for an International Driving Permit.

1-3 Months Before Move:

1. **Notify Authorities:** Notify the necessary government departments, service providers, and financial institutions in your home country about your move.

2. **Shipping Belongings:** Arrange for the shipping of your personal belongings. You might need to hire an international moving company.

3. **Utilities:** Arrange for utilities in your new home in Portugal.

4. **Bank Account:** Research how to open a bank account in Portugal.

A Few Weeks Before Move:
1. **Accommodation:** Confirm your accommodation details.

2. **Important Documents:** Gather all important documents like passports, birth certificates, and medical records. Keep these handy for your journey and initial weeks in Portugal.

3. **Farewells:** Organize farewell get-togethers with friends and family.

Upon Arrival:
1. **Registration:** Register your arrival with the local authorities, if required by your visa type.

2. **Orientation:** Take some time to get acquainted with your local area, identifying key services such as medical facilities, supermarkets, and public transportation.

Remember, these are just guidelines and may need to be adapted depending on your individual circumstances. The key to a successful move is organization and allowing yourself plenty of time to get everything in order.

13.2 What to Bring When Moving to Portugal

Deciding what to bring with you when you move to Portugal can be a challenge. Here are some considerations to help you:

Essential Documents:

1. **Passports:** Ensure that your passports are up to date.

2. **Visa Documents:** Keep all the paperwork related to your visa and immigration process readily available.

3. **Birth and Marriage Certificates:** These may be necessary for various administrative tasks.

4. **Driving License:** Your driving license, along with an International Driving Permit if required.

5. **Medical Records and Prescriptions:** These can help you to register with a doctor and get necessary prescriptions in Portugal.

6. **Education Certificates:** If you plan on working or studying in Portugal, these documents can be crucial.

Personal Items:

1. **Clothing:** Portugal has a Mediterranean climate, so lightweight clothing for summer and some warmer layers for winter should be packed. Don't forget swimwear for Portugal's beautiful beaches!

2. **Electronics:** If you're bringing electronics, check the voltage in Portugal (230V) to ensure compatibility.

3. **Home Comforts:** Items that remind you of home can help with homesickness. These could include photos, favorite books, or comfort food.

Don't Bring:

1. **Furniture and White Goods:** Unless you're sentimentally attached to your furniture, it's usually more cost-effective to buy these items in Portugal. The same goes for white goods like fridges and washing machines.

2. **Non-CE Electronics:** Electronics that don't have the CE safety mark might not be compliant with European safety regulations and might not be insurable.

3. **Certain Foods and Plants:** There may be restrictions on bringing certain types of foods, plants, or seeds into Portugal.

Remember, it's important to check customs regulations and consult with your shipping company or moving coordinator to confirm what you can and can't bring. Moreover, consider the space in your new home in Portugal and the cost of shipping versus buying new items locally.

13.3 Hiring a Moving Company for Portugal

Hiring a reliable moving company can simplify your move to Portugal significantly. Here are some considerations when selecting a moving company:

Research and Quotes:

1. **Choose Wisely:** Research several moving companies and get at least three quotes. Check reviews and ask for recommendations from other expats.
2. **Services Offered:** Consider what services are offered, such as packing, unpacking, insurance, and storage. Some companies can also assist with pet transportation or vehicle shipping.
3. **International Expertise:** Ensure that the company has experience with international moves, particularly to Portugal.

The Estimate and Contract:

1. **Inventory:** The moving company should create an inventory of your goods. This will not only determine the quote but also be necessary for customs documentation.
2. **Estimate:** The estimate should detail the costs of the move, including transport, packing services, insurance, and any additional services requested.
3. **Contract:** Review the contract carefully and understand your and the mover's responsibilities. Check the insurance coverage and the company's policy on delays, lost or damaged items.

On the Moving Day:

1. **Packing:** If you're packing yourself, use high-quality boxes and packing materials to protect your goods. Label boxes clearly with content details and which room they should be placed in.

2. **Documentation:** Ensure you have copies of all shipping documents, including inventory, insurance documents, and contact information for the moving company.

3. **Customs:** Be aware that your goods might be subject to customs inspection on arrival in Portugal. The moving company should be able to guide you through the customs process.

Remember, moving internationally can be complex. A good moving company should alleviate some of this stress, providing you with the necessary support and information to ensure your move to Portugal goes as smoothly as possible.

13.4 Banking Considerations for Moving to Portugal

Moving to Portugal involves various banking considerations to ensure smooth financial operations. Here are some important aspects to think about:

Opening a Bank Account in Portugal:

1. **Documentation:** To open a bank account in Portugal, you generally need your passport, a Portuguese

address (this can be a rental agreement or utility bill), and a tax number (NIF - Número de Identificação Fiscal).

2. **Choosing a Bank:** Major banks in Portugal include Millennium BCP, Novo Banco, and Banco Santander Totta. Research the services, fees, and account types they offer before choosing.

3. **Banking Services:** Most banks in Portugal offer online banking services, making it easier to manage your finances from home or abroad.

International Money Transfers:

1. **Costs:** Transferring money between countries can be expensive. Compare rates and fees from different services to find the most cost-effective option.

2. **Exchange Rates:** Be aware of the current exchange rates and potential fluctuations, which can impact the amount you receive.

3. **Banking Services:** Some banks or services like Wise (formerly TransferWise) or Revolut specialize in low-cost international transfers.

Managing Home Country Bank Accounts:

1. **Access:** Ensure you have online access to your home country bank accounts for any ongoing financial obligations.

2. **Taxes:** If you keep bank accounts in your home country, you may need to declare these to Portuguese authorities for tax purposes. Consult with a tax advisor to understand the implications.

3. **Direct Debits:** Review any ongoing direct debits or automatic payments. You may need to change these to your new Portuguese account.

Remember, banking regulations and procedures can change, and there can be variations between different banks. It's always best to consult directly with the banks for the most accurate and up-to-date information.

13.5 Customs Regulations for Moving to Portugal

When moving your belongings to Portugal, you'll need to adhere to the country's customs regulations. Here's a broad overview:

Household Goods:

1. **Duty-Free Entry:** Expats moving to Portugal from within the EU can typically move their household goods without paying customs duties or taxes. If you're moving from outside the EU, your used household goods may also be exempt from customs duties if you've owned them for at least six months and you plan to use them in your new residence in Portugal.

2. **Inventory List:** Prepare a detailed inventory list in Portuguese or English, indicating the items you're shipping. Some moving companies provide this

service.

3. **Prohibited Items:** Certain items, such as narcotics, weapons, and endangered animal products, are prohibited. Always check the latest regulations.

Vehicles:

1. **Importation:** If you plan to bring a vehicle, it may be subject to import taxes unless you've owned it for at least six months before moving.

2. **Documentation:** You'll need documents such as the vehicle's registration, proof of ownership, and insurance papers.

3. **Driving License:** If you're from outside the EU, you may use your home country's license for up to six months, but after this, you'll need to apply for a Portuguese driving license.

Pets:

1. **Pet Passport:** Pets from within the EU should have an EU pet passport.

2. **Vaccination and Health Certificate:** Pets from outside the EU will need a health certificate and proof of vaccinations, particularly against rabies.

3. **Microchip:** All pets must be microchipped.

Remember, customs regulations can change and can also be subject to interpretation by individual officers. Always check the most up-to-date information from official sources and consult with your moving company who will be experienced in dealing with Portuguese customs.

13.6 Notifying Home Country Government Agencies

When moving to Portugal, it's crucial to notify the appropriate government agencies in your home country to ensure a smooth transition. Here are some key entities you should contact:

Tax Authorities:

1. **Tax Status:** Inform your country's tax authority about your move to adjust your tax status accordingly.

2. **Double Taxation:** If your home country has a double taxation agreement with Portugal, you may be exempt from certain taxes in your home country. Consult with a tax advisor for specifics.

Social Security:

1. **Benefits:** If you're receiving social security benefits, notify the agency about your move. Depending on the agreement between your home country and Portugal, you may continue receiving these benefits.

Healthcare Providers:

1. **Healthcare Coverage:** Inform your healthcare provider about your move. You'll need to arrange healthcare

coverage in Portugal, but if you have ongoing medical needs, ensure you're aware of how this will be handled during the transition.

Postal Service:

1. **Redirecting Mail:** Set up a mail redirection service to your new address in Portugal, so you don't miss out on any important communication.

Election Office:

1. **Voting:** If you plan to vote in elections in your home country, you'll need to arrange to vote absentee. Contact your local election office for this.

Driver's License Issuing Authority:

1. **Driving License:** Check the requirements for driving in Portugal with your home country's license and whether you'll need an International Driving Permit.

This list is not exhaustive, and the specific agencies you'll need to contact may vary depending on your home country. It's recommended to create a checklist of all the agencies and organizations you need to notify before you move.

13.7 Relocation Services and Their Benefits

Relocating to a new country like Portugal can be a complex process. Here is where relocation services come in handy. They offer a range of services designed to make your move as stress-free as possible. Here are some benefits they offer:

1. Logistics Management:
Relocation services manage the logistical aspects of your move. This can include arranging for moving companies, coordinating shipment of your belongings, handling customs documentation, and ensuring your possessions arrive safely at your new home.

2. Local Knowledge:
Relocation companies often have extensive local knowledge, and can assist with finding suitable housing, recommending neighborhood based on your lifestyle, and even helping you navigate the local real estate market.

3. Legal Assistance:
Understanding the legal aspects of moving to a new country can be daunting. Many relocation services help with immigration, visas, work permits, and other legal processes.

4. Settling-In Services:
Once you've arrived in Portugal, the relocation service can also help you settle in. They can assist with tasks like setting up utilities, registering with local services, finding healthcare providers, and even enrolling children in school.

5. Language and Cultural Training:
For those moving to Portugal without a strong grasp of Portuguese, some relocation services offer language training. They may also offer cultural training to help you understand and adapt to Portuguese customs and etiquette.

6. Cost-Effective:

While there is a cost involved in using a relocation service, their assistance can potentially save you from costly mistakes, oversights, or logistical issues.

Choosing a relocation service is not a decision to be taken lightly. It's important to research and compare different companies, checking their reputation, the services they offer, and their fees to make sure you're getting the best service to suit your needs.